TORN ROOTS, NEW BEGINNINGS

A STORY BY MALO JAPPA

Copyright @ 2025

All Rights Reserved

Published by

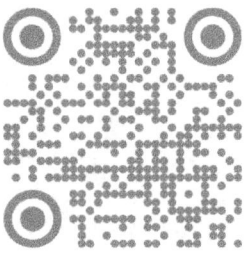

ISBN: 978-1-0689798-9-7

Table of Contents

Welcome to Canada ----------------------5

An Unexpected Opportunity --------------26

The Struggle to Find Footing--------------34

Hamza's Domestic Issues-----------------46

Pablo is the Man! -------------------------62

Pablo's Love Life is Questioned ----------71

Perfect Timing----------------------------78

The Strangest Car Ride ------------------88

A Fractured Hope------------------------111

The Breaking Point-----------------------120

A Not-So-Clean Break--------------------137

The Last Straw --------------------------150

A New Beginning-------------------------159

A Gamble for Redemption ---------------169

The Final Storm -------------------------191

TORN ROOTS, NEW BEGINNINGS

Welcome to Canada

The three men met in a way that was neither planned nor expected—three strangers drawn together by the invisible thread of shared struggle.

It was a cold morning, the kind that cut through even the thickest coats, biting at the fingers and turning breath into mist. The Service Canada office had a notice on the door that promised it would open at 9 AM sharp. But the hands of the clock had long crept past the hour, and still, the doors remained shut. A small crowd had gathered, shifting on their feet, blowing into their hands, exchanging weary glances as if to silently ask: *How long will they keep us waiting?*

Among them stood Omar, Hamza, and Pablo, three men from different corners of the world, bound by nothing but the patience of immigrants and the stubborn hope that had brought them to this land.

Hamza, his hands tucked deep into the pockets of his worn-out jacket, let out a long sigh. "Back home, if you say nine, you mean nine. Here, it seems time is just a suggestion."

TORN ROOTS, NEW BEGINNINGS

Omar chuckled, rubbing his palms together for warmth. "Oh, my brother, where I come from, if they tell you nine, they mean ten. And if they tell you ten, you'd be wise to bring lunch."

Pablo smirked, his accent rolling thick over his words. "At least where you're from, they tell you something. Back in my country, you just wait and pray that today is the day they feel like working."

The three laughed, the first crack in the ice that separated strangers from familiarity.

The cold had a way of making people talk, of forcing warmth into conversation where the sun refused to shine. They stood together, talking about the oddities of Canada, this new world where they were trying to plant their roots.

"Have you noticed how people here smile at you, but they don't mean it?" Omar asked, raising an eyebrow.

"Ah! It's true," Hamza agreed. "Where I'm from, if someone smiles at you, it means something—they want to talk, to help, or maybe even to cheat you. Here, it's just muscle movement."

Pablo nodded. "And the way they apologize for everything! You bump into them, and they say 'sorry.'"

They laughed again, shaking their heads.

"Back home," Hamza mused, "a guest is a gift from God. Here, a guest better call first, or they'll be met with suspicion."

"That's because life moves fast here," Pablo offered. "Everyone has a schedule. Back home, time belongs to people. Here, people belong to time."

Omar sighed. "*A man without his people is like a tree without roots.*"

For a moment, the laughter faded. They all knew the feeling.

Leaving home had meant leaving behind the warmth of family, the taste of childhood meals, the comfort of voices that spoke in the familiar rhythms of their mother tongues. Here, they were learning new ways to stand, to speak, to survive.

But in that moment, in the biting cold outside a government office that did not seem in a hurry to open, they found something rare and precious: understanding. The beginnings of a friendship.

A bond formed not in the warmth of shared memories, but in the cold realities of starting over.

TORN ROOTS, NEW BEGINNINGS

The doors of Service Canada finally swung open. People hurried in, eager to get their business done. But Omar, Hamza, and Pablo did not rush. They walked together, talking still, their steps lighter than before.

For the first time since arriving in Canada, they felt a little less alone.

As they sat in the waiting area of Service Canada, their conversation drifted from cultural quirks to the stark reality of life in a new country, finding work.

"They tell you Canada is the land of opportunity," Omar began, stretching his arms. "But they forget to mention you need Canadian experience to get a job. And you need a job to get Canadian experience. It's like asking a bird to fly before it has wings."

Pablo sighed, rubbing his temples. "Or like selling milk before you have a cow," he added with a bitter chuckle.

Hamza nodded, tapping his fingers against his knee. "Back home, people knew us for what we could do. Here, we are just names on a piece of paper, waiting for someone to take a chance on us."

Each of them carried a skill set that once gave them respect and purpose.

Omar, a man whose hands could bring dead engines roaring back to life, had spent years as an auto mechanic, fixing everything from motorcycles to heavy-duty trucks. If it had wheels, Omar could make it run. Back home, his reputation travelled faster than any advertisement. A broken-down car was an opportunity, not a burden.

Hamza, with his sharp eyes and steady hands, was no stranger to carpentry and construction. He could measure a beam without a ruler and tell the difference between good and bad wood with a single touch. He had built homes, bridges, and furniture that stood firm against the test of time. In his homeland, a man like him was always in demand.

And then there was Pablo, the most educated among them. A pharmacist by training, he had spent years memorizing formulas, measuring prescriptions, and advising patients on the delicate balance between medicine and health. He had walked through the doors of a hundred pharmacies, wearing his white coat like armour. But in Canada, his degree was just a framed piece of paper, gathering dust while he figured out how to make it count.

They knew the road ahead would be rough. It was no secret that newcomers often worked jobs far beneath their qualifications, swallowing their pride in exchange for survival.

"A hungry man does not refuse food just because the plate is cracked," Pablo murmured, as if reading their thoughts.

Omar nodded. *"And a wise traveller does not wait for the perfect road—he walks, even if the path is uneven."*

It was in that moment, among the faded chairs and buzzing fluorescent lights, that an unspoken agreement took shape. They might not have been brothers by blood, but in this foreign land, they could be brothers by struggle.

"If I hear about a job, I'll let you both know," Omar said, crossing his arms. "Even if it's just temporary work. We'll take what we can, build from there."

"And if I find something in construction," Hamza added, "I'll put your name forward. Sometimes, all you need is for someone to say, 'I know a guy.'"

Pablo smiled. "And if I meet someone in the pharmacy world, I'll ask what steps we need to take to make it in this new land. Maybe we find shortcuts, maybe we don't. Either way, we share information."

The agreement was simple: They would not struggle alone.

"*A single stick burns quickly, but a bundle of sticks makes a strong fire,*" Hamza said, quoting an old saying from his homeland.

They all nodded, their expressions resolute.

The clerk finally called Omar's number, snapping them out of their pact. As he rose from his seat, he looked at the other two and grinned. "No matter what happens, at least we're not starting this journey alone."

Pablo and Hamza smiled back.

The path ahead was uncertain, but now, it was less lonely.

As the three men sat outside a small café after their long wait at Service Canada, the conversation shifted to a topic they had all danced around but never fully stepped into—love.

Omar leaned back in his chair, a playful smirk on his face. "You two are family men, tied down, responsible. Me? I'm a free bird. No one to answer to, no curfews, no 'where have you been?' text messages." He chuckled, taking a sip of his coffee. "I like it that way."

Hamza raised an eyebrow. *"A bird without a nest may enjoy the sky, but when the storm comes, where does it go?"*

Pablo nodded in agreement, tapping his wedding band against the table. *"And a man who chases every butterfly finds his hands empty when winter comes."*

Omar laughed, shaking his head. "Ah, you two sound like old men already!"

Hamza and Pablo exchanged knowing glances. They had both been through the trials of commitment. Pablo's wife had been in Canada for years and was the one who had made it possible for him to come to Canada. He carried her picture in his wallet, touching it absentmindedly every time he needed a reminder of why he was here.

For Hamza, his wife and children were with him, and every dollar he earned had a purpose—rent, food, daycare, winter clothes. Back home, family was a shared responsibility; here, it was a lonely battle. He didn't talk much about it, but the tired look in his eyes spoke volumes.

Omar, despite his carefree attitude, envied them in a way he would never admit. He had freedom, yes, but freedom could feel like emptiness when no one was waiting for you at home. Still, he wore his bachelor status like a badge of honour.

"You both talk as if love is everything," Omar said, stretching his arms. "But let's not pretend marriage is easy. Tell me, does love fill the fridge? Does love pay the rent?"

Hamza exhaled, looking into the distance. "No, my friend. But when you come home tired, when the world has beaten you down, love is the hand that pulls you back up."

Pablo smiled softly. *"A man alone may run faster, but a man with a family walks further."*

Omar waved them off with a grin. "Fine, fine, you win. But I still plan to enjoy my freedom while I have it. Who knows? Maybe Canada will be good to all of us. New beginnings, new fortunes... maybe even new love."

Pablo raised his cup. "To fortune—whichever kind we may find."

Hamza and Omar clinked their cups against his, and for a brief moment, their dreams didn't seem so far away.

TORN ROOTS, NEW BEGINNINGS

For days, Omar, Hamza, and Pablo met up—sometimes at the library, other times in small coffee shops where the scent of cardamom and fresh pastries reminded them of home. They exchanged lessons learned, shared whispers of potential job openings, and kept each other's morale afloat in the turbulent sea of uncertainty.

Each of them came from different walks of life—Omar, the mechanic, whose hands were stained with grease but carried the skill to resurrect dead engines. Hamza, the carpenter, whose fingers knew the language of wood, shaping homes and furniture with quiet precision. Pablo, the pharmacist, armed with knowledge, a degree, and a frustrating realization that his credentials meant little in this new land.

"A single stick burns fast, but a bundle lasts the night," Hamza once said. He knew too well that going at it alone in a foreign country was like walking through a desert without water. The three of them, bound by circumstance, understood that their best chance at success lay in their unity.

They became each other's eyes and ears in the job market. Omar, while searching for garage work, kept an eye out for any postings that needed a carpenter or a construction hand. Hamza, when passing by a pharmacy, would step inside and ask—on Pablo's behalf—whether they were hiring. Pablo, though frustrated by his struggle to validate his degree, noted any openings in mechanical or trade work that could help Omar and Hamza.

"A rising tide lifts all boats," Pablo mused one day, remembering something he had heard before. They had all come to Canada alone, but together, they built a raft strong enough to keep them from sinking.

Their backgrounds may have differed, but their struggles were the same: the endless cycle of applications, the sting of rejection, and the unfamiliar weight of being treated as inferior simply because their experience had been gained elsewhere. They leaned on each other for support, for advice, and, most importantly, for hope.

"A man alone is prey for the wolves," Omar once muttered.

"But a pack moves with strength," Hamza added with a knowing nod.

They were no longer just three strangers who met at Service Canada. They were a brotherhood of survival, determined to carve their own space in this cold, foreign land.

And with each passing day, their dreams of stability—of belonging—felt just a little closer.

It was Pablo, the pharmacist, who first secured them a foothold in the Canadian job market—not in a pharmacy, but in a sprawling warehouse where the air smelled of cardboard and industrial steel. It wasn't the kind of work any of them had imagined when they left their homelands, but in this land of opportunity, one had to crawl before they could walk.

"A journey of a thousand miles begins with a single step," Pablo had said when he told Omar and Hamza about the opening. "It's not glamorous, but it's something."

The warehouse was a labyrinth of towering shelves stacked high with goods waiting to be shipped. Their job was simple, yet gruelling—lifting, sorting, and organizing boxes that never seemed to stop coming. The work was repetitive, the pay just enough to keep them afloat, and the shifts stretched long into the night. Yet, despite the sore backs and aching muscles, they embraced it.

"A fish may not like the water, but it cannot survive on land," Hamza muttered one evening as they clocked out, his shirt damp with sweat. He, like the others, knew that this was the price of entry. No job was too small if it meant planting roots in this new world.

Omar, always the optimist, joked that lifting boxes would at least keep them in shape. "By the time we leave this job, we'll have the arms of lumberjacks and the patience of monks."

More importantly, this job gave them something invaluable—experience. In Canada, a résumé without local work experience was as valuable as an umbrella in a hurricane. This job, no matter how menial, was their first step toward something better.

They all hoped that this warehouse would be a stepping stone—either leading to a better position within the company or serving as a bridge to something greater. They kept their eyes open, ears sharp, and resumes ready. Each shift was a chance to meet someone who might know of a better opportunity, a chance to network, a chance to move forward instead of standing still.

"A river does not cut through rock by force, but by persistence," Pablo reminded them.

And so, with tired hands but determined hearts, they carried on—lifting, sorting, and waiting for the tide to turn in their favour.

Omar had always been one to spot an opportunity in a storm. While Hamza and Pablo kept their heads down at the warehouse, hoping for a ladder to appear, Omar had his eyes on a quicker way up. He was the kind of man who could sell water to a well and still make it seem like a favour.

It wasn't long before he caught wind of the ridesharing business—a booming industry in Canada, where people always needed a quick, affordable ride. With his background in mechanics, he knew cars inside out. If he could get his hands on a vehicle, he could work on his own terms, make better money, and—most importantly—keep climbing.

But there was one problem: he needed a car, and his bank account was still gasping for air.

That's where Samantha, better known as Summer, came in.

Summer was born and raised in Canada, a woman of free spirit and easy laughter. She had met Omar at a café one evening after work, where he had flashed that confident grin of his and struck up a conversation as if they had known each other forever. He spoke with the smoothness of a seasoned storyteller, his words wrapping around her like a warm summer breeze—hence, her nickname.

She had fallen for his charm the way dry earth welcomes the first rain—eagerly, without question.

"You know, Summer," Omar had said one evening, leaning back with a mischievous smile, "a man is only as good as the wheels that carry him forward. And right now, I'm still walking."

Summer laughed. "So you're saying you need a car?"

"Not just a car—an investment," he corrected, holding her gaze. "Something that'll get me started, get us started."

She hesitated, but Omar had a way of making the impossible seem like destiny waiting to happen. He painted a picture of long-term success, of independence, of a future where he wasn't just another immigrant breaking his back in a warehouse but a man who built something for himself.

"A seed cannot grow without soil, and a dream cannot thrive without belief," he told her.

And Summer, believing in him as much as he believed in himself, agreed to help him finance a car.

For Omar, this was more than just four wheels and an engine. It was freedom. It was proof that he could carve his own path. While others waited for doors to open, he was building his own.

Omar and Summer weren't exactly official. Like a fire, love needs time to burn steadily, but Omar was more interested in the warmth than tending to the flames. He had known Summer for only a few weeks, yet with the way he spoke, he made it seem as though their connection was written in the stars.

Summer was taken in by his words and how he made the ordinary seem extraordinary. Omar was a hustler—not just in work, but in life. He knew that certainty wasn't necessary to make someone believe, only conviction.

"You and I, Summer, we're like two waves in the same ocean," he had told her one evening, looking into her eyes as if he had just discovered something profound. "We met for a reason."

It was a trick as old as time, and yet, it worked like new money.

Within days, he was behind the wheel of a car, no longer punching in at the warehouse but driving through the city, making money on his own terms. His new gig as a rideshare driver gave him the kind of freedom he craved—no bosses breathing down his neck, no repetitive tasks, no waiting for a promotion that might never come. Omar was a man who wanted movement, and now, he had it.

Hamza and Pablo weren't surprised when he left the warehouse. If anything, they saw it coming the moment he mentioned the idea. They knew Omar's nature—he was like a river, always finding a way around obstacles instead of waiting for them to be removed.

"A lion does not explain himself when he leaves the pride," Pablo had joked when Omar broke the news.

"Do what you have to do, my brother," Hamza had added with a smile. They bore no grudges—after all, wasn't the goal for all of them to climb higher?

And so, while Hamza and Pablo continued their grind in the warehouse, Omar was out on the streets, taking fares, meeting people, and living by his own rules.

To him, this was just the beginning.

Every few days, no matter how exhausted they were from long shifts or how unpredictable life in Canada had become, Omar, Hamza, and Pablo made it a point to meet. It wasn't just about catching up—it was about anchoring themselves in the storm of uncertainty that came with being new immigrants.

They would gather at a small café, a quiet park bench, or sometimes even in Omar's tiny basement apartment, where the heater barely worked. With cups of cheap coffee in hand, they would swap stories of their struggles and small victories.

"A man without a friend is like a tree without roots," Hamza would often say.

Though their backgrounds were different—Omar from Africa, Hamza from the Middle East, and Pablo from Latin America—their struggles were stitched from the same fabric. They all had left behind families, friends, familiar streets, and languages that felt like second skin. They had exchanged comfort for opportunity, certainty for a gamble. And yet, here they were, bound by the same hunger, to carve out a future in Canada that was better than the past they had left behind.

They spoke of their work—Omar's newfound freedom in ridesharing, Hamza's slow but steady climb in construction, and Pablo's quiet frustration at being overqualified for the warehouse.

"I studied for years to be a pharmacist," Pablo would sigh. "And here I am, lifting boxes instead of prescriptions."

"A man does not complain about the darkness; he lights a candle," Hamza would remind him, nudging his friend to stay hopeful.

Omar, always the smooth talker, would grin. "Pablo, my brother, we just have to find you the right hustle. Even the tallest trees started as seeds."

They laughed, they vented, they encouraged one another. Theirs was a friendship not built on convenience, but on survival. In a land where they were nameless faces in a crowd, they were each other's family. And as long as they had each other, they had something to hold onto.

Omar rarely spoke about his personal life, not because he had none, but because the weight of his responsibilities was too heavy to toss into conversation casually. In his culture, a man did not complain—he endured. He wore his struggles like an iron vest beneath his charming exterior, never letting anyone see the burden pressing down on him.

Back home, his parents and younger siblings depended on him. Every dollar he earned in Canada

TORN ROOTS, NEW BEGINNINGS

stretched across borders, feeding mouths, paying school fees, and keeping a roof over their heads. To fail in Canada would mean more than personal disappointment; it would mean plunging his family back into hardship.

"A man is not measured by the size of his wallet, but by the number of people who depend on him," his father had told him before he left. That lesson clung to him like a shadow, never letting him forget why he was here.

Even as he laughed with Hamza and Pablo, flashing his signature grin, he was mentally calculating remittances, expenses, and the ever-growing gap between what he had and what he needed. Every ride he drove, every tip he pocketed—it all had a purpose beyond himself.

"Omar, you always look so relaxed," Pablo once remarked. "Like nothing bothers you."

Omar chuckled, sipping his coffee. "My friend, *the ocean looks calm on the surface, but only the fish know how strong the current is.*"

Hamza, ever perceptive, tapped him on his shoulder. "Just remember, even a camel needs to rest. *Don't break yourself before you make yourself.*"

Omar simply smiled. He didn't have the luxury of slowing down. The road ahead was long, and there was no turning back.

An Unexpected Opportunity

The money was better, no doubt about that. Despite the instability of working in the gig economy, Omar felt a newfound sense of control over his life. No boss hovering over his shoulder, no fixed hours chaining him down. He could weave through the city streets as he pleased, turning his car into a vessel of opportunity, picking up stories as much as he picked up passengers.

Every ride was a glimpse into a different Canada. Some riders were indifferent, treating the country as nothing more than a colder extension of the world they knew. "Canada? It's just another place to work and pay bills, my friend," one passenger scoffed, staring out at the gray streets.

Others, however, spoke of the country like poets reciting verses of love. "Canada is not just a country—it's a promise," an elderly man told Omar one evening. "A place where the son of a cashier can become a doctor. A place where winter may be harsh, but opportunity is warm."

These words stirred something in Omar. He had come seeking fortune, but maybe Canada could offer him more than just a paycheck. He found himself eager to learn, absorbing the stories and perspectives of every person who entered his car. Some were born here, some were immigrants like him, and each one carried a different shade of the Canadian dream.

He shared these encounters with Hamza and Pablo whenever they met up. "Some people say Canada is nothing special. Others act like it's paradise," he mused one night.

Hamza chuckled, adjusting his coat. "*A river is only as good as the fish that swim in it. Some thrive, others complain about the current.*"

Omar nodded. He was determined to be the kind of fish that thrived.

It was a cold evening, and Omar's car smelled faintly of the spiced tea he had picked up earlier. The hum of the engine mixed with the occasional chatter of the radio, but the real story unfolded in the backseat.

His rider, a middle-aged man with the weariness of responsibility etched into his face, let out a sigh. "People think Canada is a land of endless opportunity," he mused. "And it is—but opportunity means nothing if you don't have the right people to seize it."

Omar glanced at him through the rearview mirror. "You sound like a man who's had his share of struggles."

The rider let out a dry chuckle. "You don't know the half of it, my friend." He ran a hand through his graying hair. "I run a construction business, but keeping it afloat is like carrying water in a woven basket. Labour shortages are killing us. Everyone wants work, but no one wants to work."

Omar's ears perked up. Construction. That was Hamza's trade. And while Pablo was a pharmacist by profession, he had made it clear that for now, he was open to anything. Omar himself wasn't afraid of hard work. A man with responsibilities back home couldn't afford to be picky.

"Tell me about the job," Omar said, his voice steady.

The rider leaned forward, sensing the flicker of interest. "It's basic work—carpentry, site cleanup, some heavy lifting. Pay isn't bad, and if you're good, there's room to grow."

Omar pressed further, asking about pay, conditions, and whether experience was a requirement. With each answer, his confidence grew. "You and your friends sound like just the kind of people I need," the man admitted.

By the time they reached the rider's destination, they had exchanged numbers. The man, hopeful to fill his labour shortage, extended his hand. *"If you're serious, you can start next week. Bring your friends. I promise you won't regret it."*

As Omar shook his hand, an old saying came to mind: *"A single chopstick breaks easily, but a bundle is strong."* He knew that alone, he could take the job and earn some money, but together with Hamza and Pablo, they could truly build something—if not in construction, then in their own journey toward success.

That night, when Omar met up with his friends, his eyes gleamed with opportunity. Fate had given them a door. Now, all they had to do was walk through it.

Omar sat in his car, engine idling, fingers drumming rhythmically on the steering wheel. The offer from his last rider weighed on his mind like a stone in his pocket—small, yet impossible to ignore. He already had a job driving, and while it wasn't perfect, it gave him freedom. His heart, however, belonged under the hood of a car, hands deep in grease and metal, reviving engines with the precision of a surgeon.

"*A man should follow the path of his footprints,*" he murmured to himself. His dream was still to work as a mechanic, not to haul bricks and hammer nails.

Yet, this wasn't just about him. This was the kind of job Hamza had been praying for. He had arrived in Canada with the smell of sawdust still clinging to his clothes, his calloused hands eager to grip a hammer again. Construction was his trade, his bread and butter, and a chance like this was not to be taken lightly.

Then there was Pablo. The man with the mind of a scientist but the patience of a labourer. He had spent years studying pharmacy, yet here in Canada, his degree sat on the sidelines, waiting for validation. Would he take the job? Omar wasn't sure. Pablo might be willing to roll up his sleeves, but deep down, he was searching for something more aligned with his expertise.

"*A bird does not refuse a seed just because it dreams of fruit,*" Omar thought. Even if this job wasn't his path, it could be a stepping stone for one of his friends. And in life, a man must recognize the difference between what is good for him and what is good for his people.

Omar called Hamza and Pablo in a group call. He wasted no time. "Boys, I found something," he began, his tone measured. "It's not for me, but it might be for you."

Hamza's eyes lit up instantly, and even Pablo listened with interest. Omar smiled to himself. If he couldn't use the opportunity, at least it wouldn't go to waste. They talked about meeting up later to discuss the job offer in detail, as Omar was still working.

Fate, it seemed, had a way of knocking twice in one day. No sooner had Omar wrapped up his conversation about the construction job than another rider slid into the backseat, bringing with him the scent of opportunity—quick, elusive, and tantalizing, like the smell of fresh bread just out of reach.

This new rider, a man with the air of someone who knew the shortcuts in life, leaned forward as the car rolled through the dim city streets. "You're new here, aren't you?" he asked, his voice smooth as silk.

Omar chuckled, adjusting the rearview mirror to meet the man's gaze. "That obvious?"

"Brother, you still got that hunger in your eyes—the kind that only fresh immigrants have. You want to make it, and you want to make it fast."

Omar grinned, always eager to hear what people had to say. He could talk to anyone, and more often than not, he could turn even the most serious face into a smiling one. His words danced in conversations like a street performer flipping a coin between his fingers—effortless, dazzling, and disarming.

"Well, tell me then, what's the quick way to make a buck?" Omar asked, half-joking but fully interested.

The man smirked, leaning back against the seat. "There are ways, my friend. Ways they don't tell you about in those newcomer brochures. Some just require knowing the right people."

Omar's curiosity was piqued. He had come to Canada with an open mind and a hustler's spirit. In his world, opportunity was like water—it could slip through your fingers if you weren't ready to catch it.

"I like meeting the right people," Omar replied, his voice light but his mind working fast.

The rider nodded approvingly. "Then follow up with me, and maybe I'll introduce you to a few doors that open faster than others."

As Omar dropped him off, he watched the man walk away, his words lingering in the air like a whispered promise. A new job lead in one hand, the hint of another opportunity in the other—it had been a good day.

But in a land of plenty, not all doors lead to fortune. Some can lead to ruin.

The Struggle to Find Footing

Omar had always been a man with his hands in many pots—one foot on solid ground, the other testing the waters. When the construction job came through, he wasn't entirely sold on it, but Hamza and Pablo had a way of pulling him in.

"Brother, this is how we build something real," Hamza had told him, wiping dust from his forehead after their first day. "A job with a schedule, a paycheck that doesn't depend on luck. It may not be forever, but it's a start."

Pablo had chimed in, ever the logical one. "We need to plant roots before we can grow. This work isn't glamorous, but at least we know the money will come."

Omar nodded, knowing they meant well. And so, he joined them, swinging hammers by day and keeping his little secret by night. A fisherman never reveals all his nets, and Omar wasn't about to show all his hands.

MALO JAPPA

Every morning, he showed up on site, ready to mix sweat with concrete, but when the sun set, he had other business. The quick-money scheme from the smooth-talking rider had him intrigued, and he had started dipping his toes into something else— something he wasn't ready to talk about just yet.

Not because he didn't trust his friends, but because he knew how they would react. Pablo, with his measured approach to life, would call it reckless. Hamza, a man who had a family depending on him, would tell him not to gamble with his future.

So Omar kept his mouth shut, smiling through their long days of labour, knowing that when the time came, he would decide for himself which road to take.

A man with too many roads ahead must choose wisely, for not all paths lead home.

It is said that *when the sun shines too brightly, a storm is never far behind*. Just as Omar, Hamza, and Pablo were settling into a routine, the winds of misfortune swept through.

The construction company that had promised stability crumbled under financial strain. One morning, the workers arrived only to find the gates locked and a simple notice taped to the door: **"Operations** suspended until further notice." The whispers among the workers turned into a chorus of frustration. Some cursed their luck; others simply sighed, already accustomed to life's unpredictability.

For the three friends, it was a familiar lesson—in life, no tree grows straight; the wind bends us all in different directions.

Hamza clenched his jaw, already calculating his next move. Pablo adjusted his jacket, ever composed but visibly disappointed. Omar, however, took it in stride. He had always believed that a man who knows many trades never goes hungry.

"Boys, we'll figure something out," he said, trying to keep the mood light.

That evening, as they sat together discussing their next steps, Omar made an offer. "Look, until we get something else, let me help you guys out. No shame in it. We're brothers in this."

Hamza shook his head with a wry smile. *"A man who relies too much on his friend's kindness will forget how to stand on his own."*

Pablo patted Omar's shoulder. "We appreciate it, hermano. But we're not there yet. We'll make it through."

Omar sighed, understanding their pride. He knew that *a hand stretched too often for help would soon forget how to make a fist.* They had come to this country to build something of their own, and that meant enduring the hardships that came with it.

So, with nothing but their hunger for a better future, they went back to the drawing board. The job hunt resumed, but each of them knew—Canada was not a place for the faint of heart.

It is said that *a river that has never known obstacles does not know its strength.* Omar, however, was in no hurry to test his limits—at least not in the way his friends were.

While Hamza and Pablo spent their days scouring job postings and knocking on doors, Omar was living a life of adventure. He had figured out the secret to getting by—keep your feet in many places, but never let your roots settle too deep.

His rideshare gig had opened doors to a lifestyle he never imagined. Each week brought new women, new places, and new experiences. From the neon-lit streets of Toronto to the coastal charm of Vancouver, Omar was on the move, often with a different woman by his side. If there was a party, he was at the center of it; if there was a thrill, he was the first to chase it.

Meanwhile, Summer was caught between love and reality. She had fallen hard for Omar's charisma, the way he could turn the dullest moment into something magical. She told herself that *a young man's feet must dance before they find the rhythm of home.* Perhaps, if she gave him enough space, he would grow out of his wild ways and come back to her.

But deep down, she knew. Omar was a wind that refused to be bottled.

At first, she tried to ignore the signs—the last-minute cancellations, the disappearing acts, the vague explanations. But with time, the truth became clear: Omar was not looking for something permanent, at least not yet.

Still, she hoped. "Maybe he just needs time," she told herself. "Maybe he has to get it all out of his system before he realizes what really matters."

But as the old saying goes, *a bird that has tasted the sky does not long for a cage.*

MALO JAPPA

It is often said that *a man without work is like a tree without roots*—weak, vulnerable, and at the mercy of the winds of fate. Hamza, once a proud provider, now felt like he was losing his footing in the very land he had sacrificed everything to reach.

Back home, his family had lived comfortably. He had made a name for himself as a skilled carpenter, and his wife had never worried about where their next meal would come from. But Canada had proven to be an unforgiving teacher, and the lessons were coming at a steep price.

The construction job had barely lasted long enough for them to find their rhythm before the company folded, leaving him back at square one. The job boards were barren, the agencies had no callbacks, and even the odd cash jobs were drying up. What had once been a hopeful journey now felt like a slow descent into despair.

At home, his wife was growing resentful. "You promised me a better life," she reminded him, her voice heavy with disappointment. "But what kind of life is this?"

Hamza had no words. What could he say? A man does not build a house only for the rain to seep through the cracks. He had poured his entire fortune, his very being, into this dream. But now, that dream was unravelling, and his wife's patience was wearing thin.

She had once been his greatest supporter, the woman who stood by his side through thick and thin. But the weight of uncertainty was changing her. The whispers of regret had turned into arguments, and the warmth in her eyes was slowly being replaced by frustration.

"Back home, at least we had dignity," she said one evening, as they sat in the dimly lit apartment. "Here, we are beggars waiting for luck to knock on our door."

Hamza swallowed hard. *A man's pride is like a glass — once cracked, it is never the same again.* He could feel the weight of failure pressing against his chest, suffocating him.

And yet, he could not give up. He had made a vow—to his wife, to his children, to himself. He would find a way, no matter what it took. A drowning man does not stop swimming just because the shore is far.

"A house where the man has no work is like a pot with a hole —no matter how much you pour in, it will never be full." This thought haunted Hamza as he lay awake at night, staring at the ceiling, listening to the rhythmic breathing of his sleeping children.

Sara had found a job shortly after they arrived in Canada. It was not glamorous—just a retail position that barely covered rent and groceries—but it was something. At first, she had been patient, reminding herself that Hamza was trying his best. But patience wears thin when hunger and stress set in.

At the end of every month, their bank account teetered on the edge of empty, and every dollar had to be stretched. "How long are we going to live like this?" Sara would ask, her voice tight with exhaustion.

Hamza felt the sting of those words like salt on an open wound. *A man's honour is in his ability to provide*, but what honour was left when he had to watch his wife carry the entire household on her back? He wanted to tell her that he was doing his best, that things would turn around, that he would find something. But empty promises tasted bitter on his tongue, and he had already made too many of them.

At work, Sara masked her struggles with a smile, but at home, the cracks were beginning to show. The woman who had once been his partner in dreams now looked at him with quiet resentment. She had sacrificed everything to start a new life with him, and now, she was the only one keeping it afloat.

TORN ROOTS, NEW BEGINNINGS

One evening, after another long shift, she sat at the dinner table, staring at the bills stacked in front of her. The children had been put to bed, and the silence between them was heavier than the air before a storm.

"I'm tired, Hamza," she said finally, her voice barely above a whisper.

"*I know,*" he replied, looking down at his hands, rough from years of carpentry, now idle and purposeless.

"No, you don't," she snapped, frustration spilling over. "I go to work, I come home, I take care of the kids, and I do it all over again while you—" She stopped herself, shaking her head.

Hamza clenched his jaw, feeling the shame curl in his stomach. He wanted to yell, to defend himself, to remind her that he had been looking for work every day, that he had taken every odd job he could find. But what was the point?

A man who cannot provide is like a bird with clipped wings—he may still look strong, but he cannot fly.

Sara sighed, rubbing her temples. "I just... I just want to know that things will get better. Because I don't know how much longer I can do this."

Hamza reached for her hand, but she pulled away. The distance between them was growing, like a crack in the foundation of a home that no one had the strength to repair.

Outside, the cold Canadian night stretched on, indifferent to their struggles. Hamza closed his eyes and whispered a silent prayer—because at this point, what else did he have left?

"A man who finds a good wife has found a treasure, and a home filled with love is richer than a palace with gold."

Pablo and his wife, Camila, had built their little sanctuary amid the chaos of their new life in Canada. Unlike Hamza and Sara, whose struggles were weighing them down, Pablo had the rare fortune of a wife who was his pillar of strength. While he had yet to find stable employment, Camila had taken up the role of provider without resentment, carrying their household on her capable shoulders.

"Don't worry, *mi amor,*" she would say, pressing a gentle kiss to his forehead. "We are a team, and we will figure this out together."

Pablo knew he was lucky. Many men in his position would have faced bitterness and blame, but Camila had a heart as vast as the ocean—patient, nurturing, and unshaken by the storms of life. She worked long hours at her job, coming home exhausted yet still finding the energy to fill their home with warmth.

Their apartment was small, modest, but full of love. The scent of her cooking—garlic, cumin, and freshly baked bread—filled the air, wrapping Pablo in comfort even on his worst days. He would sometimes feel the weight of not being able to contribute financially, but Camila never made him feel less of a man.

Instead, they focused on their dreams—one dream in particular. They had been trying for a child, eager to start the next chapter of their lives. Pablo had imagined it so many times: a little one with Camila's kind eyes and his mischievous smile, laughter filling their home like music. But despite months of trying, there was no baby.

"Maybe it's just not the right time," Camila would say, always the optimist.

But Pablo felt the quiet ache in his heart. He didn't voice it often, but he sometimes lay awake at night, wondering if life was playing a cruel trick on him. He had left behind his career as a pharmacist, his home, and his familiar comforts, and now even the one thing he longed for—a child—seemed just out of reach.

"*Dios tiene un plan,*" Camila would remind him. "*God has a plan.*"

Pablo clung to her words, because if he let doubt take over, he feared it would drown him. In the meantime, he poured his love into their relationship, grateful for the woman beside him. After all, *a man who is loved is never truly poor.*

Hamza's Domestic Issues

"A house divided against itself cannot stand."

Sara had always been outspoken. Back home, her voice carried weight, her opinions shaping decisions in a household that had never known struggle. But in Canada, her words were edged with exhaustion, frustration curling around every syllable like smoke from a dying fire.

"I didn't leave everything behind just to struggle like this, Hamza," she snapped one evening, slamming a pot onto the stove harder than necessary. "You said things would be hard at first, but we've been here for months, and we are still barely surviving."

Hamza clenched his jaw. He had heard these complaints before, but each time they stung like salt in an open wound.

"I am trying, Sara. You think I don't feel it? You think I don't know what I've done?" He gestured around their small apartment, nothing like the spacious home they had left behind. "I brought my family from comfort to struggle. I know that. But what do you want me to do? Pull money from thin air?"

Sara sighed, running a hand over her face. She wasn't cruel; she knew Hamza was trying. But it wasn't enough. Back home, they lived comfortably, not luxuriously, but good enough to not worry about tomorrow's bills. Here, they were counting pennies, living paycheck to paycheck, constantly worried about rent.

"You work a few days here and there, and then what? It's not stable. The kids need stability, Hamza. I need stability."

Hamza felt the weight of her words pressing on him like a boulder. A man is supposed to provide; that's what his father had taught him. *"A man without work is a man without honour."* And yet, here he was, scraping by with odd jobs, unable to give his family the security they deserved.

He loved Sara, but these arguments were becoming unbearable. Every night felt like another battle, each word a knife twisting in his gut. He wanted to scream that he wasn't some lazy fool sitting around waiting for a handout. He was up at dawn, searching, applying, doing whatever work he could find.

But in Sara's eyes, it wasn't enough.

One night, after another argument left them sitting in bitter silence, Hamza stepped out onto their tiny balcony. The city lights stretched before him, vast and indifferent. He had given up everything to be here, believing in the promise of a better future.

But was it really better?

"A man who carries too much weight will eventually stumble," he muttered under his breath.

For the first time since arriving in Canada, Hamza felt like he was at his breaking point.

"An empty sack cannot stand upright."

Hamza spent his days scouring job boards, calling old and new contacts, and checking in with Omar and Pablo to see if they had heard of anything. But the answer was always the same—a sigh, a shake of the head, a muttered "nothing yet."

Omar, ever the hustler, was making money through his rideshare gig and whatever side opportunities he could find. Pablo, cushioned by his wife's steady income, wasn't in a rush. But Hamza? He was drowning, and no lifeboat was in sight.

At home, the air was thick with unspoken words, every moment between him and Sara stretching like a rubber band about to snap. The children were too young to fully grasp the tension, but they felt it—how their mother's voice was sharper, how their father's laughter had disappeared.

Sara barely spoke to him unless it was about bills. She came home tired, dragging her feet, her face carrying the weight of their struggles. One evening, as they sat at the dinner table in heavy silence, she finally broke.

"You need to figure something out, Hamza," she said, her voice calm but firm. "This isn't sustainable."

Hamza clenched his fist under the table. "You think I don't know that?" He wanted to say more, but what was the point? He had no answers, no solutions.

The nights grew colder, not because of the weather, but because the warmth between them had started to fade. The tension coiled in the air like a viper, ready to strike at the slightest movement.

"A man without work is like a tree without roots," Hamza whispered to himself as he stared at the ceiling that night. He knew something had to change—*and soon.*

"The dog barks, but the car moves on."

TORN ROOTS, NEW BEGINNINGS

Hamza's frustration was becoming a simmering pot, its contents threatening to boil over. Sara's threat hung like a dark cloud over him, casting a shadow on every interaction. He knew she had reached the edge, and he was teetering on the same precipice.

The conversation started one evening, after another long day with no job prospects. It was one of those nights where everything felt heavier—the house seemed smaller, and Sara's eyes, usually filled with concern, were now tinged with resentment.

"Hamza, I can't do this anymore. I can't keep living like this. I didn't come here for this." Her voice trembled, but there was an undeniable strength in her words. She wasn't asking; she was telling him. Telling him to fix things—or else.

The ultimatum hit him like a fist to the gut.

"If you don't find something soon, I'm going back home. I can't raise the kids like this. You promised me a better life. Where is it?"

Those words echoed in his mind. *Better life.* He had promised her everything. *A future of comfort and success,* but here they were, struggling in a cold, foreign land with no safety net.

"I'm not going anywhere," Hamza snapped, his voice low but steady, the anger rising in his chest. He wasn't about to let her just walk out and leave him behind. Not when he had already sacrificed everything.

Sara's hand clenched around the edge of the table. "I will, Hamza. I will leave if you don't do something about this. I can't keep doing this alone."

It was the last straw. He could feel the tension pulling between them, thick like rope, ready to snap.

Hamza, driven by desperation, stood up quickly, pacing around the room. His eyes darkened, and for a moment, something in him faltered. He felt the weight of the frustration, of the mounting pressure to fix everything. *Everything was on his shoulders.*

And then, a thought crossed his mind—his family back home. If he didn't succeed here, he would become a disgrace. He would fail in the eyes of everyone who had supported him. No, he could not let that happen.

He looked at Sara, his face reddened with anger, but there was something else there—a deep well of regret. He could feel the heat of his frustration rising, but he knew that violence, even in a fleeting moment, was not an option. *"A hand raised in anger is the first step toward ruin,"* he told himself, the proverb echoing in his mind.

He'd seen men lose everything to a single reckless act. The thought of being deported for domestic violence, to lose everything, made him pause.

Instead, he took a long breath and pushed the rage down, his voice shaking with barely contained fury.

"I'm doing everything I can, Sara. I know this is not what we planned. I know things aren't working out the way we hoped, but I swear I will fix this. I will find something. I'll do whatever it takes, but I will not let you leave."

Sara, eyes narrowed, saw the struggle in his face, but it wasn't enough. Her expression softened, but the tears in her eyes told a different story. It wasn't just about the money; it was about the trust, the love, the feeling of being abandoned in a strange land, carrying the family on her shoulders alone.

She stood up slowly, her shoulders heavy. "I don't want to leave, Hamza, but I can't keep waiting for you to change. I don't know how much longer I can hold this all together."

Hamza stood there, helpless, his mind racing. What else could he do? How could he fix this when everything seemed to be falling apart? His anger had given way to something far more devastating—fear.

Fear of losing his family. Fear of failing. Fear of being the man he never wanted to become.

As Sara walked out of the room, her back turned to him, Hamza couldn't help but wonder if he was losing everything in the same way the rest of his life had unravelled—one piece at a time.

The air in Hamza's small apartment was thick with tension, heavy enough to cut through with a knife. Sara's eyes were fiery with frustration, her words cutting through the silence like a storm. Hamza stood on the other side of the room, his fists clenched, his heart racing with the bitterness of helplessness.

Their fight had reached its boiling point when the doorbell rang unexpectedly, breaking through the chaos like a light piercing through a darkened sky.

Hamza's face was tight with anger as he glanced at the door, ready to lash out, but then the reality of the situation hit him—it was Pablo.

Pablo, ever the level-headed one, had arrived just in time.

He stepped inside with his usual warmth, greeting them both with a smile that, for a brief moment, seemed to disarm the tension in the room. He could sense immediately the heaviness hanging between them. Sara's face was streaked with tears, her shoulders hunched as she fought to contain the avalanche of emotions crashing down on her. Hamza stood rigid, as though trying to hold himself together by sheer force of will.

Pablo, without missing a beat, walked into the living room and set down the bag of groceries he'd brought with him. He wasn't there to pick sides, and certainly not to add fuel to the fire. He had been through enough himself to know that sometimes, words were more powerful than silence, and patience far more effective than anger.

"Hamza, Sara..." Pablo began, his voice calm but firm. "This isn't you."

Hamza, still seething, looked at Pablo with frustration etched into his face. He wanted to say something—anything—but the words wouldn't come. The pressure of everything mounting on him seemed to have locked his mouth shut.

Sara, with a deep sigh, wiped her eyes. She had stopped shouting, but her frustration hadn't dissipated. It lingered, settling in her bones like a heavy ache.

Pablo took a step closer, his eyes locked onto both of them, his gaze steady but compassionate. "I know this isn't easy for either of you," he said. "But fighting like this, it's only going to tear you both apart."

Hamza's shoulders slumped a little, his anger turning into exhaustion. He had tried so hard to make it work. He had believed in the promise of a better life here, but it seemed like the harder he fought, the more he lost. And Sara, the woman he loved, the mother of his children, was slipping away.

"But we can't just keep waiting," Sara spoke up, her voice quieter now, yet still sharp. "We came here to make something of ourselves, Hamza. I came here for our girls. But I'm struggling... I need to see progress. I need to know we're not stuck."

Pablo nodded solemnly, understanding the weight of her words. He, too, had come to Canada with dreams of a better life. But he knew well enough that the path wasn't easy, and more often than not, it was an uphill climb.

"I know it's difficult, Sara. But remember, you both came here for a reason. You came here for your daughters. This place offers them a future that you couldn't give them back home. A future where they can grow up free of the burdens you both faced."

Sara's eyes softened at the mention of their children. "I want them to have more than we did. But every day it feels like we're sinking."

Pablo turned to Hamza then, his voice gentle but with a strength behind it. "Hamza, I know you're doing everything you can. And I know you're scared. But if you lose hope, you lose everything. Your family, your future. And worst of all, you'll lose each other. Don't let that happen."

There was a pause, the weight of Pablo's words hanging in the air. Hamza felt something stir within him—hope. It was a fleeting thing, like a bird just beyond reach, but it was there. And for the first time in days, he found himself grasping for it.

"What do you think we should do?" Hamza asked, his voice thick with exhaustion, but a trace of genuine curiosity lacing his tone.

Pablo smiled softly, stepping closer to both of them. "You both need to remind yourselves why you came here. Don't let the weight of the struggle cloud the vision you have for your family. It's not just about surviving, it's about finding ways to thrive together. Don't lose sight of that."

He looked at Sara and then at Hamza, his eyes filled with understanding. "It's hard right now. But you can't let it tear you apart. Your daughters are watching you, and they will grow up seeing how you both handled this—together."

Sara bit her lip, nodding slowly. She hadn't realized how much her frustration had clouded her vision. In her mind, she had only seen the struggle, the never-ending cycle of disappointment. But she understood now—they had to keep fighting, together.

Hamza's face softened. He had been so caught up in his fears and failures that he had forgotten what really mattered: *his family*. The family he had fought so hard to build.

"You're right, Pablo," Hamza said quietly. "I've been too focused on what I've lost, and I haven't been paying attention to what we still have. We have each other. We can get through this. Together."

Pablo's expression softened as he nodded. "That's the spirit. Hold on to that. Don't let anything, not even the weight of this new life, pull you apart."

With a deep breath, Sara looked at Hamza, her eyes no longer filled with frustration but with a renewed understanding. She wasn't just a partner in the struggle; she was a partner in hope. And in that moment, hope was all they needed.

The room, which had once been filled with tension and anger, now seemed to settle into a quieter space, one of quiet resolve. With Pablo's guidance, they had found their way back to each other, to the reason they had come to Canada in the first place: for their children, for their future.

"We'll get through this," Hamza said, his voice stronger now, full of conviction. "Together."

And for the first time in a long while, Sara truly believed him.

Pablo knew that sometimes, all it took was a few words and a fresh perspective to change someone's mindset. After helping to calm things down inside, he pulled Hamza aside for a quick chat. They stepped outside into the cool night air, the dim streetlights casting long shadows over the sidewalk. Hamza's shoulders were still heavy with the weight of his worries, but Pablo could sense that beneath the frustration and exhaustion, there was something more —*hope*, though buried deep.

"Listen, Hamza," Pablo said, his voice calm but firm. "This isn't the end for you. You're just in a bad spot right now. You have a family, you have people who care about you. Don't let pride and fear swallow that. Sometimes, you need to lean on the people around you to lift yourself."

Hamza stood still for a moment, processing Pablo's words. He had been so focused on surviving that he'd forgotten what it meant to fight *together* with his wife. It wasn't just about finding a job, it was about staying connected, about remembering what they had fought for in the first place.

"You're right, Pablo. I've been caught in my head too much," Hamza admitted, his voice tinged with a sense of relief. "I've been so focused on what's not working, I forgot about what is working—Sara, my daughters, and... the opportunity we came here for."

Pablo gave him a reassuring pat on the shoulder. "It's easy to lose sight of that. But remember, tough times don't last, but tough people do. You've got this, Hamza. Don't let the fear of failure take your family down with you."

Hamza took a deep breath and nodded. His mind was clearer now. It was going to be hard, but he could handle it—*they* could handle it.

When they returned inside, Hamza walked into the living room with a noticeable change in his demeanour. His posture was less slumped, his face less clouded with stress. Sara looked up from where she had been sitting, her eyes tired but hopeful.

"I'm sorry, Sara," Hamza said softly. "I've been so focused on everything that's wrong that I didn't see how much we still have. I promise, I'm going to do better. We're in this together."

Sara's face softened, her relief palpable. She reached out and touched his hand, grateful for the man she had married, the man who had just found his way back to her.

"Thank you," she whispered, squeezing his hand gently. "I just want us to find a way to get through this."

As the night settled in, Pablo stood up to leave, a quiet smile on his face. He had done what he set out to do. He had reminded Hamza and Sara of the strength in their unity, and of the love that would carry them through even the hardest times.

"Take care of each other," he said, his voice full of sincerity. "You'll get through this. One day, you'll look back and be grateful for how far you've come."

With that, Pablo walked out the door, disappearing into the night, leaving Hamza and Sara standing together in the warmth of their small home, the tension between them slowly fading into something more hopeful, more resilient.

Pablo is the Man!

The next morning, the three men met as they usually did, their usual spot at a small café that had become their unofficial meeting place. The air was still crisp, carrying the scent of freshly brewed coffee and warm pastries. Hamza arrived first, looking better than he had the previous night, though the weight of his struggles still clung to him. Omar strolled in next, his usual swagger intact, despite his hidden burdens. But it was Pablo who stole the moment.

He walked in with an undeniable energy, his grin wide and his eyes gleaming with the kind of excitement that only comes when life finally throws you a lifeline. *Hope is the best seasoning for any meal*, as they say in many cultures, and today, Pablo was serving it in abundance.

"Boys, I have some good news," he announced, clapping his hands together before sitting down. "I found work for all of us."

Hamza and Omar leaned in, eager to hear more.

"It's not glamorous, but it's steady," Pablo continued. "My wife's friend works in logistics and mentioned

MALO JAPPA

they need hands in a distribution warehouse for a large construction company. The pay is decent, and it's something to keep us going while we figure out our next moves."

Hamza exhaled, his relief evident. After weeks of uncertainty, this was exactly what he needed—stability, even if temporary. Omar, though less enthusiastic about warehouse work, nodded. He wasn't one to turn down an opportunity, and he could always keep working on his side gigs.

"That's not all," Pablo added, his grin widening. "My wife also told me about a process to get my pharmacist license here in Canada. If I stay focused, I can finally get back into my profession."

Omar chuckled, shaking his head. "So, what you're saying is that while we break our backs in a warehouse, you'll be studying to become a big-time pharmacist, huh?"

Pablo laughed. "Hey, we all have to start somewhere. But listen, this is a win for all of us. A foot in the door is better than standing outside in the cold."

Hamza, who had been quietly listening, finally spoke. "Pablo, you have no idea how much this means to me.

To us." He glanced at Omar, who nodded in agreement. "We'll take it."

A sense of camaraderie settled between them, reinforcing the unspoken pact they had made to support one another. As the old Swahili saying goes, *'Unity is strength, division is weakness.'* They weren't just three men trying to make it in a foreign land—they were brothers in struggle, bound by hope and the belief that brighter days were ahead.

Pablo raised his coffee cup. "To new beginnings."

Omar smirked, raising his own. "To not breaking our backs in that warehouse."

Hamza laughed, shaking his head before lifting his cup. "To better days."

They clinked their cups together, sealing the moment with laughter and optimism. No matter what lay ahead, they knew one thing for certain: they were in this together.

The trio started their new jobs with the construction company specializing in building houses. It wasn't glamorous, but it was steady, and in a land where opportunity often came disguised as hard work, they knew better than to turn it down.

From the moment they started, Hamza proved to be an invaluable asset. His background in carpentry and construction meant that he wasn't just another pair of hands—he was skilled, efficient, and knowledgeable. Their general manager quickly took notice, praising Hamza's craftsmanship. *"A good worker is worth more than gold,"* the boss often said, nodding in approval as Hamza effortlessly cut and measured wood, his hands moving with the precision of an artist sculpting a masterpiece.

Pablo, though unfamiliar with the trade, was adaptable and willing to learn. He worked diligently, knowing that every dollar earned brought him closer to getting his pharmacist license. He viewed this job as a stepping stone, reminding himself of an old Spanish saying, *"Poco a poco, se anda lejos"*—little by little, one goes far.

Omar, on the other hand, was stretched thin. Between his ridesharing job, construction work, and an ever-expanding nightlife, he was burning the candle at both ends. He was the first to wake up and the last to go to sleep, running on adrenaline and ambition. Yet, despite the exhaustion, he couldn't bring himself to slow down. "Sleep is for the rich," he joked whenever his friends warned him about his gruelling schedule.

TORN ROOTS, NEW BEGINNINGS

At night, while Hamza went home to his family and Pablo studied for his future, Omar was out—dressed sharp, moving from club to club, meeting new women, and living for the moment. His life was a whirlwind, and he thrived in the chaos, always chasing the next thrill.

But as the old African proverb goes, *"However long the night, the dawn will break."* Omar was riding high, but how long could he keep up the pace before something gave way?

Hamza's troubles at home were growing like weeds in an untended garden—fast and overwhelming. No matter how much he worked, it never seemed enough. The money he brought home was swallowed up by rent, bills, and the endless needs of a growing family. Sara was running out of patience, and Hamza felt the weight of his failure pressing down on him like an unshakable burden.

"A man without money is like a bow without an arrow," his father used to say back home. And in this foreign land, Hamza felt utterly disarmed.

He barely had time to hang out with the boys anymore. When he did, Sara's sharp words echoed in his mind, demanding to know why he was out instead of finding ways to bring in more money. "What's the point of struggling in Canada if we're just surviving? We had a better life back home!" she would say. Hamza knew she wasn't wrong, but going back wasn't an option—not when they had sacrificed everything to be here.

At work, he was a valuable man. On the construction site, his skills were respected, and his work was steady. But when he walked through the front door of his apartment, none of that seemed to matter. He saw only the stress in Sara's eyes and the growing resentment in her voice.

Hamza feared that his home was already beginning to crack, and if things didn't change soon, the walls would come tumbling down.

Pablo had always been the responsible one, the steady hand in the trio. But with Camila working long hours and their home feeling emptier than he had expected in this new life, he found himself drawn to Omar's carefree energy.

At first, it was just an occasional evening. Omar would invite him out after work, and Pablo would hesitantly agree, telling himself he wouldn't stay out too late. But one night turned into another, and soon, he found himself getting comfortable in a world that was completely foreign to him.

TORN ROOTS, NEW BEGINNINGS

"A man is known by the company he keeps," his mother used to warn him back home. Yet, there was something exciting about being around Omar. Pablo had spent so much time worrying about stability, about finding his footing, about building a future. Omar, on the other hand, seemed to dance through life with ease. He charmed people effortlessly, moved from one thrill to the next without hesitation.

Omar had a saying for everything. *"Life is short, hermano! If you're always waiting, you'll die waiting."* Pablo couldn't argue with that.

The loud music, the flashing lights, the endless laughter of women whose names he barely remembered—it was all so different from the careful life he had always lived. He didn't even drink much, but he still felt intoxicated by the energy of the night.

Deep down, Pablo knew this wasn't him. This wasn't the life he had planned. But in that moment, with Omar leading the way, it felt good to forget the stress, to forget the pressure of expectations, to just exist.

For the first time in a long time, Pablo wasn't thinking about tomorrow.

At first, Camila didn't question it. She understood that Pablo was under a lot of pressure—working long hours during the day, studying to reclaim his pharmacist license at night. If he needed to unwind, who was she to deny him that?

But twice a week turned into a habit. Pablo would come home later and later, his excuses always wrapped in reason. "It's just a couple of drinks, mi amor. Nothing serious." Or, "Omar and I are just catching up. He's been through a lot, too."

Camila had always known Pablo to be a responsible man, one who weighed every decision with care, like a pharmacist measuring out the perfect dose of medicine. But now, something was changing. She noticed the way he avoided her eyes when she asked where he had been. She noticed the way he laughed differently, lighter, and distant.

"You can't expect to plant corn and harvest wheat," her grandmother used to say back home. Camila knew that spending too much time with Omar would lead Pablo down a path he might regret.

One night, as Pablo was getting ready to leave, she stood in the doorway with her arms crossed. "Is this winding down, or are you escaping?" she asked softly.

TORN ROOTS, NEW BEGINNINGS

Pablo hesitated, just for a second, before flashing that reassuring smile she used to love. "Come on, Camila. You know me."

Yes, she did. That's what worried her.

Pablo's Love Life is Questioned

Camila had always trusted Pablo. He was the kind of man who kept his word, who followed through on his promises. But now, something was different. The man who once burned the midnight oil poring over pharmacy textbooks was now burning through his nights in bars and clubs.

At first, she convinced herself it was nothing. *"Let him have his fun,"* she thought. *"He works hard; he deserves to let loose."* But fun had a way of turning into habit, and habit into trouble.

Pablo came home later each night, the scent of alcohol clinging to him like a second skin. His laughter, once full of warmth, became careless, hollow, the laughter of a man who was avoiding something. And then there were the nights he didn't make it home on his own.

More than once, Omar would drag him in, his arm slung over his friend's shoulder, barely able to stand.

"Your man had a little too much tonight," Omar would say with a grin, as if this were all just part of the game.

Camila would force a smile, thank Omar, and put Pablo to bed. But as she pulled off his shoes, covered him with a blanket, she would wonder: *Who is this man? Where did my Pablo go?*

She had always been patient, but patience had its limits. And one night, as Pablo stumbled through the door again, she finally asked:

"Is this who you are now?"

Pablo blinked at her, his face flushed from alcohol. He opened his mouth to respond, but no words came. Camila didn't need an answer. She already knew.

Camila had always believed that love, like a well-tended garden, needed constant care—watered with attention, warmed with affection, and pruned of neglect. Yet, no matter how much effort she poured into reviving their romance, Pablo remained distant, like a ship drifting further from shore with each passing tide.

At first, she blamed herself. *"Maybe I've been too consumed with work,"* she thought. *"Perhaps he feels alone."* In an effort to bridge the growing gap, she took time off, eager to rekindle what once felt effortless. But love is not a plant that revives simply because the gardener wills it—sometimes, the roots have already withered.

She prepared his favourite meals, hoping the familiar taste of home would stir old affections. She suggested walks in the evening, recalling how they once held hands under the city lights, whispering dreams of a future together. But Pablo was no longer the same man. He would come home late, shrug off her attempts at conversation, and when she suggested they spend time together, he would rush her out the door with a distracted kiss on the forehead.

"A house with no warmth is just four walls," her grandmother had once told her. And now, she felt it—cold creeping into the spaces where love had once lived.

Pablo was slipping away, and Camila, despite all her efforts, was losing her grip.

Camila had never been one to shy away from the truth. She believed that *a wound ignored only festers* and that it was better to rip off the bandage than let doubt eat away at her. So, with determination in her step and fire in her heart, she sought out Omar.

TORN ROOTS, NEW BEGINNINGS

Omar, ever the smooth talker, initially tried to deflect. He chuckled, shrugged, and made vague comments about how *"men just need to blow off steam sometimes."* But Camila wasn't one to be brushed aside. She crossed her arms, fixed him with a gaze sharp enough to cut through excuses, and demanded honesty.

Omar respected Camila—not just as Pablo's wife but as a woman who had built her life in Canada from the ground up, brick by brick, before bringing Pablo over to share in her dreams. He couldn't lie to her, but neither could he betray his friend. So, he took a deep breath and chose his words carefully.

"Pablo is struggling, Camila. He's got a lot on his mind, and he's using alcohol to quiet it down. He's not himself. But whatever's wrong, it's not because he doesn't love you."

It wasn't the full truth, but it was the most he could give her without breaking Pablo's trust. Camila, though unsatisfied, nodded slowly. *"A drowning man reaches for anything,"* she murmured, her voice heavy with worry.

When Camila realized that Omar would not betray Pablo's confidence, she chose to respect his loyalty, even though it frustrated her. *"A secret is like a stone in the shoe—small but painful,"* she thought, but she knew that forcing answers wouldn't help. Instead, she resolved to find the truth on her own.

The next day, when Omar and Pablo met up, Omar wasn't his usual carefree self. He wasn't laughing, wasn't making jokes, and most importantly, he wasn't suggesting they hit the clubs. Instead, he leaned in, his voice serious.

"No partying tonight, Pablo. We need to talk."

Pablo raised an eyebrow but didn't protest. Omar, usually the one keeping things light, had a different energy about him today.

"Listen, man," Omar continued, lowering his voice. "I can't keep going like this. Things are getting serious with Summer, and also getting complicated. And... I need to be real with you. Your drug use is getting worse. I thought you had control over it, but the truth is, it's starting to control you."

Pablo exhaled sharply, looking away. He had been avoiding his problems, drowning them in alcohol and reckless nights, but now Omar's candid assessment made it impossible to ignore the truth—*he was spiralling.*

"This life we're living, bro… it's not sustainable. We came here for better, didn't we? But look at us." Omar's voice was firm but laced with regret.

Pablo didn't answer right away. He just sat there, staring at the table, as if seeing their choices laid out in front of him for the first time.

Omar leaned in closer, his voice unwavering. "Listen, bro, out of respect for Camila, you need to talk to her. She deserves the truth. If you don't, the next time she asks me, I'm telling her everything."

Pablo clenched his jaw, running a hand over his face. He knew Omar wasn't bluffing. Loyalty among friends was one thing, but Camila had earned her place in their circle. She had sacrificed for him, built a life for him to step into, and now, he was repaying her with deception.

"I'll talk to her," Pablo finally said, his voice low.

"No, man," Omar shook his head. "Not just talk—be real with her. No excuses, no brushing it off. You owe her that."

Pablo sighed deeply. He had been avoiding this moment, hoping things would fix themselves, but life didn't work that way. "Alright. I promise."

Omar nodded, satisfied but still concerned. *"Good. Because if she asks me again, I won't lie for you."*

Pablo swallowed hard. The moment of reckoning had come.

Perfect Timing

Omar had always been a hustler, and selling drugs was just another extension of his natural ability to connect with people and make things happen. He wasn't the kind of dealer lurking in the shadows—his charm made him a favourite among partygoers and club regulars. He moved through the scene effortlessly, his wide smile and easygoing nature making him more of a "social fixer" than a street-level criminal. People didn't just come to him for the product; they came for the experience, the conversation, the illusion that they were special because Omar, the ever-popular and charismatic man, was giving them attention.

The money was pouring in faster than ever, and Omar embraced the lifestyle with open arms. The nights were longer, the drinks flowed freely, and the women were drawn to him like moths to a flame. Every evening felt like a scene out of a music video—fast cars, high-end clubs, and an entourage that followed him wherever he went. Yet, in the back of his mind, he knew how dangerous the game was. There was an old saying back home, *"He who climbs a thorn tree must be ready for scratches."* Omar was riding high, but he also knew that a single misstep could send everything crashing down.

Summer, ever hopeful, still believed that he was going through a phase. She convinced herself that Omar was simply enjoying the rush of youth, that this wild streak was something he needed to burn through before settling down. *"A river may twist and turn, but it still finds its way to the ocean,"* she told herself, convinced that Omar would eventually return to her, ready for the quiet life. But deep inside, she knew she was lying to herself. His late nights, the secretive phone calls, and the expensive gifts that appeared without explanation were signs she could no longer ignore.

Meanwhile, Omar was growing more reckless. The more successful he became, the bolder he got. He started taking bigger risks, trusting people he shouldn't, and slipping into the dangerous illusion that he was untouchable. His clients weren't just club kids anymore—some were serious players, people with connections to the kinds of men who didn't forgive mistakes. The higher he climbed, the more precarious his position became. *"A man who dances with fire must expect his feet to burn,"* but Omar was too caught up in the thrill to slow down.

Pablo had been walking the straight and narrow for weeks, trying to shake off the habits that had begun to erode the foundation of his marriage. He had cut back on the wild nights, distanced himself from the reckless lifestyle, and put his focus back on his studies. Camila had started to relax, believing that the storm had passed. She saw glimpses of the man she had fallen in love with—the one who had dreams bigger than parties and ambitions stronger than temptation.

Then, Omar called.

It was an invitation to a high-profile party, the kind where money flowed like water, and indulgence was the main attraction. Omar, ever the persuasive talker, pitched it as just a night out. "Come on, hermano," he said smoothly, "It's just one night. You need to breathe a little. You can't study forever."

Pablo hesitated. He had been doing so well, keeping his head down and focusing on the future. But something about Omar's words stirred a longing in him. The truth was, he missed the thrill—the energy of the nightlife, the feeling of being surrounded by people who laughed too loud and lived too fast. *A bird that has once tasted the wind finds it hard to stay in a cage.*

Camila, ever watchful, sensed his inner struggle. "You've worked too hard to throw it all away," she reminded him, her voice gentle but firm. "You said you were done with all of that."

Pablo smiled, pulling her into his arms. "I am, mi amor. I just need a break, one night to let loose. I can control myself." His words were confident, but the devil always waits for a crack in the armour.

Camila wasn't convinced, but she also didn't want to be the reason he felt trapped. He had been good—no late nights, no disappearing acts, no waking up with regrets. Maybe, just maybe, he had grown stronger. And so, with a sigh, she kissed him on the forehead and let him go. *Even the strongest tree bends when the wind is persistent enough.*

Pablo walked out the door, promising himself that he would only stay for a while, that he would drink lightly, that he would stay far from the shadows he had worked so hard to escape. But temptation doesn't announce itself with fanfare—it slithers in quietly, like a thief in the night, waiting for the perfect moment to strike.

And Omar, whether he realized it or not, was leading his friend straight back into the lion's den.

The night had started with good intentions, as so many nights do. The boys were feeling invincible, the music pulsed like a heartbeat, and the air was thick with expensive perfume and the scent of mischief. Pablo had convinced himself that this was just another social event—an opportunity to rub shoulders with the right people, to make connections that could help him in the medical industry. He had dressed the part, spoken with the right amount of confidence, and kept a firm grip on his soda, determined to prove to himself—and to Camila—that he could handle a night out without slipping.

But temptation has a way of dressing itself in the sweetest disguises.

She was stunning, the kind of woman who turned heads effortlessly. She moved through the party like she belonged to a world where indulgence was second nature. When she approached Pablo with a playful smirk and a drink in hand, the weight of his promises suddenly seemed lighter.

"Just one," she coaxed, pressing the glass into his hand.

Pablo hesitated, the words *"I don't drink"* balancing on the tip of his tongue. But the music was too loud, the night too young, and her gaze too expectant. *A man who stares at the sun too long is bound to go blind.*

He took the drink.

One became two. Two became four. The warmth spread through his body, numbing the stress, blurring the lines between responsibility and recklessness. The laughter came easier, the conversations more effortless. He told himself he was still in control—that he could stop anytime he wanted. But control is an illusion in the presence of old vices.

Before long, the lines between fun and destruction disappeared entirely. The woman led him further into the party, where the drinks were stronger and the temptations heavier. He gave in. One bad decision led to another, and soon he was doing everything he had sworn to leave behind—drugs, excess, the chaotic spiral of a man who had once promised himself he would never be this weak again.

Meanwhile, Omar was too caught up in his revelry to notice Pablo slipping away. He had seen his friend talking, laughing, and moving through the crowd with ease. He assumed Pablo was fine—after all, he had been the one resisting temptation all night. But the devil moves quietly, and Pablo had already lost the fight.

It wasn't until someone shouted his name that Omar realized something was wrong.

TORN ROOTS, NEW BEGINNINGS

Pablo was passed out, his body slumped in the corner, his breathing shallow. The room spun around him, but he was no longer conscious enough to feel it.

Omar's heart pounded as he pushed through the sweaty crowd, his mind torn between two conflicting thoughts. He had just seen a woman who looked eerily like Hamza's wife, Sara. It couldn't be, could it? He had only met her a handful of times, but something about the way she moved, the familiar sharpness in her gaze, made his stomach churn with unease. *"No, I'm imagining things,"* he told himself. *"I have bigger problems right now."*

Pablo was barely conscious, his head lolling forward as Omar hoisted him up. "Come on, bro, we gotta get out of here," he muttered, trying to keep his voice low. He could feel the weight of Pablo's body dragging against his own, making it difficult to move through the dense crowd.

People were still dancing, laughing, oblivious to the storm brewing just outside the doors. But Omar's instincts were screaming at him—*leave now.*

Half-carrying, half-dragging Pablo, he made his way outside, searching for the first available taxi. The air was thick with smoke and the faint scent of something burnt lingered. Just as he was about to step into the street, a swarm of red and blue lights flashed in the distance. His breath caught in his throat.

Police.

The realization hit like a gut punch. He could already hear the officers yelling as they stormed the building, their voices cutting through the night like a blade. The partygoers inside were oblivious, dancing on a sinking ship.

Omar moved fast, shoving Pablo into the back of a taxi and slamming the door shut behind them. He barked the first address that came to mind—Pablo's place—and the driver took off just as chaos erupted behind them.

He turned to look out the rear windshield as the flashing lights grew brighter, people spilling out of the house in a frantic rush. The timing had been too close—seconds later, and he might have been caught in the raid.

As the taxi sped through the dark streets, Omar clenched his fists, his heart still hammering. He wasn't a religious man, but in that moment, he prayed.

Prayed for being spared.

Prayed that Pablo would be okay.

And, against his better judgment, he prayed that the woman he saw *wasn't* Sara. Because if it was... then things were about to get a whole lot worse.

When they arrived at Pablo's home, Camila opened the door, her face a mixture of relief and dread. The moment her eyes landed on Pablo's limp form, barely able to stand, her breath hitched in her throat. Before she could ask any questions, Omar blurted out the only truth he could bring himself to say.

"I think Pablo's an addict... and he needs professional help."

The words hung in the air, thick and heavy. Camila didn't respond. Instead, she nodded numbly and stepped aside, allowing Omar to carry Pablo inside. She moved on autopilot, helping Omar lay him gently on the bed. The weight of reality pressed down on her, and before she knew it, her legs gave out, and she collapsed onto the floor.

Silent at first, then with shaking shoulders, she broke down in tears.

Omar sighed, rubbing his face with his hands. He had seen heartbreak before, seen people crushed under the weight of their circumstances, but something about this moment made his chest tighten. Camila had sacrificed everything for Pablo—moved from the only country she had called home, worked tirelessly, and built a life for them both. And now, here she was, watching the man she loved unravel before her eyes.

He sat beside her on the floor, unsure of what to say. Words had little comfort in moments like these. Instead, he did what he knew best—he stayed.

For the rest of the night, Omar made sure Camila didn't spiral too deep into her emotions. He sat with her when the sobs became too much. He reassured her when the guilt threatened to consume her. He watched over Pablo, checking on him every so often to make sure he was sleeping properly.

By the time dawn broke, the house was silent. Pablo was still asleep, Camila had finally cried herself into an exhausted slumber on the couch, and Omar sat staring out the window, his mind racing.

This wasn't just a bad night.

This was the beginning of something much worse.

The Strangest Car Ride

Just as dawn broke, Omar's phone buzzed relentlessly, shattering the fragile quiet that had settled over the house. He groggily reached for it, rubbing the exhaustion from his eyes as he answered.

"Omar, I need a ride. It's an emergency," Hamza's voice was tight, urgent, the kind of tone a man uses when the ground beneath him is crumbling.

Omar sat up, instinctively alert. "Where are you?"

Hamza gave him an address, and without another word, Omar grabbed his keys and slipped out the door. He wasn't in the mood for more trouble, but trouble didn't ask for permission—it came like a thief in the night, unannounced and unwelcome.

When he pulled up, Hamza was already outside, pacing, his face drawn in worry.

"What's going on?" Omar asked, watching as Hamza climbed into the car, his hands wringing together like a man praying for a miracle.

"It's Sara," he exhaled heavily, his voice thick with shame. "She went out with some friends last night and got arrested at the party."

Omar's grip on the steering wheel tightened, his mind flashing back to the woman he had seen the night before—the familiar face he couldn't quite place in the chaos of Pablo's downfall. His stomach twisted. He knew. He had seen her there.

But now was not the time for confessions.

He swallowed his thoughts and simply nodded, pulling the car onto the road. The silence between them was thick, heavier than the morning fog that clung to the streets.

Hamza was unravelling in the passenger seat. His foot tapped restlessly against the floor, his breath uneven.

"How did this even happen?" Omar finally asked.

Hamza scoffed, running a hand over his face. "She said she just needed a break, needed to get out. I didn't think much of it. Then I got a call from her saying she was at some house party when they raided it."

Omar didn't respond.

TORN ROOTS, NEW BEGINNINGS

He knew the game too well—people looked for escape where they could find it. Hamza had been drowning under the weight of expectations, and Sara had been suffocating in disappointment. She wanted the life she had before, and when it didn't come, she reached for something else, anything else.

It was an old story, one he had seen too many times.

In his grandmother's village, they used to say, "*A drowning man will clutch at a snake if he thinks it can save him.*"

Sara had clutched at the wrong thing.

As they pulled into the police station's parking lot, Hamza let out a long breath. "Omar, do me a favour, man. Don't tell anyone about this. I don't need people talking."

Omar looked at him, really looked at him, before nodding. "I got you."

Because at the end of the day, loyalty is a man's last currency. And in a world where everything else could be lost, that was the only thing that mattered.

The wait for Sara to be processed felt eternal. The air in the police station was thick with the stench of sweat and stale bureaucracy, the kind of place where time moved differently, slower, heavier.

Finally, the doors opened, and Sara stepped out, her eyes darting around nervously before landing on Hamza. She looked like a woman who had been dragged through the depths of her worst nightmare, yet the relief of seeing her husband was immediate.

"I'm so sorry," she whispered, her voice fragile, barely holding itself together. "I didn't mean for this to happen."

Hamza exhaled sharply, rubbing his temples. "Let's just go home," he muttered, too exhausted to say anything else.

As they walked out, Sara stole a glance at Omar, and for the first time, she really saw him. Her face paled. The same hoodie. The same jeans. The same man from last night.

Her steps slowed.

Omar caught it immediately—the slight hesitation, the panic in her eyes. He knew what was coming before she even opened her mouth.

Hamza excused himself to visit the restroom just as Sara turned to Omar, her voice desperate but hushed. "You saw me there, didn't you?"

Omar didn't respond. He just watched as she wrung her hands, the shame dripping from her like water from a leaky faucet.

"Please," she pleaded, eyes glossy with unshed tears. "Hamza can't know. It would break him."

Omar exhaled. He didn't owe her anything. But he understood.

Hamza and Sara's marriage was already on shaky grounds—one more crack, and it might crumble completely.

"Don't worry," he said finally, his voice steady. "This stays between us."

Sara's shoulders sagged in relief. "Thank you."

By the time Hamza returned, neither of them spoke of what had just transpired. The secret had already been buried, locked away between them.

As Omar drove them home, the weight of the night pressed against his chest.

Some truths, he realized, were best left unspoken.

Omar kept his hands on the steering wheel, his mind running circles around Sara's words.

He had only seen her drinking—nothing more. A simple drink, something that didn't seem out of place at a party. But the way she had pleaded with him, the desperation in her voice, told a different story.

Why would she ask him to keep quiet unless there was something worth hiding?

He stole a glance at her through the rearview mirror. She was staring out the window, lost in thought, her fingers intertwined tightly in her lap. Hamza, on the other hand, sat in the front seat, his leg bouncing with nervous energy.

Omar had been around enough people living double lives to know when something wasn't adding up. He had seen men and women unravel under the weight of their secrets.

Something about last night wasn't sitting right.

Had Sara been drinking something stronger? Had she been with someone she shouldn't have been? Had she done something that could wreck her marriage?

TORN ROOTS, NEW BEGINNINGS

Omar didn't know.

But now, thanks to her fear, he knew there was more to the story than what met the eye.

For Omar, it was becoming a puzzle, a challenge that tickled his curiosity. He had always been good at reading people, seeing past their façades to the truth hidden beneath. But this wasn't just any riddle—it was one that could unravel the fragile threads holding his friends' lives together.

He looked at Hamza, who was sitting beside him, his shoulders slumped with the weight of his struggles. Omar knew that Hamza was fighting battles on multiple fronts—his pride, his work, and the mounting pressure of supporting a family that had once lived in comfort, now scraping by in Canada's tough job market.

The man's entire world had been turned upside down. From the grandeur of his home country to the harsh realities of life as an immigrant, Hamza had sacrificed everything for his family. The thought that the one person he trusted most in this new life could be the one to betray him weighed heavily on Omar's heart.

Omar didn't want to believe it. There was a saying in his culture: *"The truth always comes out, like the sun that rises no matter how dark the night."* It was a reminder that everything hidden eventually surfaces, but also that people—good people, even—deserved the chance to mend their mistakes before they were torn apart by their secrets.

"What if Hamza's family could stay intact?" Omar thought. *"What if there was another explanation for Sara's actions?"*

But his instinct, honed over the years from countless experiences, told him that there was more to this story than anyone was willing to say. And he couldn't shake the feeling that, somewhere deep down, Sara was hiding a truth that could break Hamza.

The more Omar thought about it, the more he realized that the stakes weren't just high for Hamza. They were high for him, too. He was embedded in this web of relationships, and any wrong move could send everything spiralling into chaos.

Still, he couldn't ignore the suspicion gnawing at him. The thought that Hamza's wife could no longer be trusted—*that* was the part that unsettled him the most. No matter how deep he buried his concerns, he couldn't shake the image of Hamza, broken and betrayed, sitting alone at home, questioning everything he had worked so hard to rebuild.

TORN ROOTS, NEW BEGINNINGS

Omar's eyes darted to the rearview mirror again. Sara sat in silence, her face blank, her thoughts hidden behind an unspoken wall. He didn't know if she was guilty, or if it was just his own growing suspicion, but one thing was certain—he wasn't going to let this go.

For now, though, the best he could do was hold on to his loyalty to Hamza. He didn't have the whole story, and he wasn't about to jump to conclusions. But as the wheels turned under his feet, the puzzle pieces slowly began to fall into place. It was only a matter of time before everything would be revealed.

The phone rang only once before Omar picked up using the car's bluetooth, oblivious to the impending doom. Pablo's anger boiled over the moment Omar answered his phone, his voice seething with frustration. Pablo's voice was sharp and accusing, cutting through the silence like a knife.

"What the hell, Omar?!" he shouted, his words filled with betrayal. "Why the hell did you spend the night with my wife? What happened? What did you do while I was sleeping?"

Omar's heart sank as he listened to his friend's outburst. He hadn't expected this kind of reaction. Pablo's insecurities had always been simmering beneath the surface, and now they were bubbling over, threatening to drown everything in a wave of mistrust.

"I didn't do anything, Pablo," Omar said calmly, his voice steady. He could hear the tension in Pablo's breath on the other end. "I was there to make sure Camila didn't lose it. She was upset, and I was just looking out for her, man."

But Pablo was having none of it. The accusations continued to pour out of him, each one more wild than the last. "I don't buy it, Omar. You think I'm stupid? You think I don't know what's going on? You and Camila—two of you—taking advantage of my problems, getting rid of me while I'm in rehab so you can have a free run at each other!"

His words hit Omar hard, a punch to the gut. He never imagined Pablo would think that way. But then, in Pablo's state of mind, full of guilt and paranoia over his addiction, it made sense. Everything was twisted, seen through the lens of his addiction and his sense of inadequacy.

"No, Pablo," Omar pleaded, trying to calm his friend down. "You've got it all wrong. Camila has been trying to get you help for weeks. This wasn't about us. This was about you. She's worried about you, and I'm just trying to be a friend. I want you to get clean. I want you to get out of this mess."

But the more Omar spoke, the more Pablo's mind spun with doubt and jealousy. The idea that Camila had suggested rehab didn't sit right with him. It felt like a final decision—a sign that everyone was ready to move on without him. In his twisted, foggy state, rehab was just a way to take him out of the picture, to remove him from the equation entirely so that Camila and Omar could finally be together.

"You're lying, Omar. I know exactly what's going on. I'm not stupid. You've been hanging out with her, spending time with her, and now you're going to get me out of the way? You both just want me gone, don't you? You want my wife, my life... You think you're doing me a favour, but all you're doing is pushing me away."

Omar sat still, fighting back the sting of hurt that welled up in his chest. He knew Pablo had always been self-conscious, especially when it came to his drug use. But this was different. This accusation cut deeper than anything he had ever heard before.

"Pablo, listen to me. We're all in this together. Camila is doing this because she loves you. She wants you to get better. I want you to get better. But you've got to trust us. I'm not after your wife. I'm not trying to take your place." Omar took a deep breath, trying to make his voice sound as sincere as possible. "You've got to trust Camila, man. And you've got to trust me. This is about your recovery, not about me and her."

But Pablo wasn't listening. His mind was too clouded to be rational about something he considered the ultimate betrayal. The notion of his wife wanting him to go to rehab had only confirmed his worst fears—that she was ready to move on without him. That she was tired of dealing with him.

"I don't believe you, Omar," Pablo snapped, his voice trembling with a mixture of anger and hurt. "You've already made your choice; I can see it now. I'm just a pawn in your little game. Go ahead, take her. You'll have her all to yourself soon enough. But don't think for one second that I'll ever forgive you."

The line went dead before Omar could say another word. The weight of Pablo's accusations hung over him like a dark cloud. He couldn't believe it had come to this. He had tried to be there for Pablo and help him see that Camila only wanted what was best for him. But Pablo had twisted the whole situation into something ugly and unrecognizable.

TORN ROOTS, NEW BEGINNINGS

Omar couldn't help but feel a pang of guilt. He knew that the road to healing for Pablo was going to be long and hard, but he never imagined it would cost him the trust of his friend. But Pablo wasn't seeing things clearly right now, and Omar hoped—prayed—that one day he would.

For now, though, there was nothing more Omar could do but wait, hope, and perhaps, in time, prove that his loyalty to Pablo had never wavered.

Omar stood at a crossroads, his mind racing with conflicting emotions. The weight of the situation pressed heavily on his chest, like a thousand-pound boulder he couldn't lift. The bond he shared with Pablo, once unbreakable, had been shattered, leaving a jagged crack in the friendship that had once felt invincible. Yet, despite everything, Omar couldn't bring himself to walk away. Not from Pablo. Not from Hamza. They were his friends, his brothers in arms, and no matter how bad things got, that was something he couldn't easily sever.

It was as if he were standing in the middle of an intersection, unsure which way to go. To the left, the path of loyalty beckoned him, urging him to stand by his friends, to put everything else aside and prove that his friendship was unwavering. But to the right, the path of self-preservation whispered a quieter, more tempting promise—freedom from the chaos, freedom from the emotional weight of being the glue that kept their shattered lives together.

But Omar couldn't shake the thought that, if he walked away now, he'd be abandoning them at their lowest. There was no going back from that. A person could leave a broken friendship behind, but the regret of not trying to mend it would gnaw at his conscience forever. As the old proverb goes, *"A friend in need is a friend indeed."* Omar had always believed in that simple truth, and as much as he wanted to escape the constant turmoil, he knew he couldn't turn his back on the people who had grown to see as his family.

Yet, as seconds passed, the situation became increasingly volatile. It was like a ticking time bomb, the fuse already halfway burnt. Each minute, the tension grew more unbearable, like a tightrope Omar had been walking, with no safety net beneath him. He could feel the strain of balancing his friendship with Pablo and Hamza while still trying to salvage his life and mental health. The proverbial weight on his shoulders grew heavier with each street light they passed, but somehow, he pressed on.

There were moments when he would think about walking away, about cutting ties and focusing solely on his own future. The temptation was strong. After all, they hadn't made it easy for him. Hamza's volatile behaviour, Pablo's downward spiral into addiction, and the constant drama were more than enough to drive anyone to the edge. Yet, whenever he thought about leaving, he remembered the vows they'd shared, the times they'd supported each other through thick and thin. *"A friend's true worth is revealed in times of trouble,"* another proverb whispered to him, reminding him that loyalty wasn't just about the good times—it was about standing by each other through the bad.

Omar knew he couldn't walk away yet. Not now. Not when they needed him most. Despite all the cracks in their lives, despite the emotional toll it was taking on him, he couldn't abandon his friends in their darkest hours. He wasn't one to give up so easily, and he wouldn't start now.

But the more he thought about it, the harder it became to consider walking away. His own life—his jobs, his dreams, his relationship—were beginning to slip through his fingers like grains of sand. The constant tension was like an invisible weight that was starting to wear him down. It was as if he were trapped in the middle of a storm, the wind howling in his ears, the rain battering him from all sides, and yet he couldn't bring himself to leave the shelter of his friends.

He thought about the old saying from his grandmother: *"You can't change the direction of the wind, but you can adjust your sails."* The winds of chaos were blowing around him, and while he couldn't stop the storm from raging, he could choose how to navigate it. He could stay the course, try to help them as best he could, or he could turn away and focus on his own survival.

But even then, Omar wasn't sure if there was a right answer. All he knew was that, for better or worse, he was tied to these men. And no matter how much he might wish to step away, to escape the bomb that was bound to explode, his heart and his conscience told him that leaving wasn't an option. Not yet.

At the end of the day, Omar wasn't sure what the future held. He couldn't predict how the situation would unfold or whether things would improve or worsen. But he did know one thing: *"A tree is known by its fruits,"* and if his friends needed him to be the roots holding everything together, then that was a responsibility he would bear, no matter the cost. The road ahead was uncertain, but Omar had made his choice. He wasn't going to walk away. Not now. Not when they needed him the most.

The tension in the car was palpable, thickening the air with each passing second. Omar's call with Pablo had been unsettling, the raw emotion and accusations hanging between them like a fog. Sara and Hamza, sitting quietly in the car, exchanged glances but didn't speak. The car was filled with an uneasy silence, broken only by the hum of the engine and the occasional turn of the wheel. A ride that could've taken only 10 minutes was taking them more than an hour in Toronto traffic, but Omar had gotten used to that as a rideshare driver.

The phone call had ended with nothing more than a few gruff words exchanged, but its impact lingered. Omar's voice, strained with the effort to keep calm, had done little to hide the undercurrent of frustration that had been building between him and Pablo. And now, as the call ended and the conversation fizzled out, the silence among the three of them felt deafening. No one knew what to say, not even Omar, who typically had a way with words.

As the car made its way down the street and then into the driveway, Hamza and Sara were finally home. The tires crunched against the gravel as they came to a stop. Without a word, Sara gathered her things and opened the door. She had her own life to attend to— her mess to sort through—and wasn't in the mood for small talk.

The silence that followed was almost suffocating. Hamza and Omar sat still, neither of them eager to break the silence. When Hamza stepped out of the car and walked toward the building, it was as if a door had closed behind him, one that neither of them dared to open.

"Well," Hamza said as he joined Sara before walking into their home, his voice low and measured, "this isn't over, is it?"

Sara didn't respond immediately. She let the question linger in the air like smoke that couldn't be cleared. Finally, with a deep sigh, she spoke, her voice tinged with frustration. "I don't know, Hamza. I really don't. But I'm starting to think maybe we all need a break from each other for a while."

Hamza didn't reply. He stared ahead, not wanting to acknowledge what Sara had said, but knowing deep down that it was true. The strain between them had been growing for months, and it was becoming harder to ignore. Yet, for all the unspoken words and unresolved tensions, neither of them knew how to break the cycle they had found themselves in.

As Omar made his way up to the front door, the sound of his footsteps echoed in the quiet house. The moment he entered, he was enveloped by the normalcy of his surroundings—everything was still and familiar. He sighed deeply, closing the door behind him, grateful for the silence but already dreading the inevitable storm that would follow this uneasy truce. The weight of the conversation with Pablo, coupled with his own internal struggle, hung over him like a dark cloud.

He had always known that his friendships with Pablo and Hamza would come with their fair share of complications. But now, as he moved through his day, he couldn't help but wonder how much longer he could carry the burden of their problems. Would the cracks in their lives eventually break open, or would they all manage to somehow keep things together, despite it all?

The days would feel uncertain, and while Omar couldn't predict the future, one thing was clear: the path he was on wasn't just about loyalty to his friends anymore. It was about surviving the fallout of their choices—and his own.

Omar stood at a crossroads, caught in a whirlwind of conflicting emotions. The weight of loyalty to his friends, combined with the growing realization of his role in their lives, felt almost unbearable. It was as if he were walking a tightrope, the delicate balance between standing by his friends and preserving his integrity shifting with each passing day.

As he sat in the quiet of his home, the stillness only amplified the turmoil brewing within him. He had always believed in the value of friendship, that bonds were formed through shared struggles, triumphs, and the unspoken promises to stand by one another. But now, it seemed that every decision he made pushed him further into a moral grey zone, where the lines between right and wrong, loyalty and honesty, were beginning to blur.

Pablo had always been his closest friend. Their bond had been forged through months of shared experiences, laughter, and hardships. But lately, their relationship had become strained. Omar had stood by as Pablo's life unravelled, silently bearing witness to the spiral of drug use and deception. He had given advice, offered support, and tried to be the friend he thought Pablo needed. But now, as the cracks in their friendship deepened, Omar wondered if he had failed in some fundamental way.

Then there was Hamza, who had been desperate to rebuild his life after arriving in Canada, trying to find his place in a foreign land. His struggles, though different, were no less real. Hamza's family had come to rely on Omar for support, whether it was a ride, a loan, or sometimes babysitting. But as Omar watched Hamza's marriage fray under the weight of financial strain and uncertainty, he began to question his role in all of this. Was he meant to be the steady friend who picked up the pieces every time things fell apart? Or was he just an enabler, perpetuating the cycles of dysfunction by allowing them to lean on him too heavily?

Then there were the wives—Camila, who had been struggling with Pablo's addiction, and Sara, whose frustration with Hamza's inability to provide for their family had pushed her to the brink. Omar's relationship with them had always been that of a concerned bystander, someone who offered support but never truly understood the depth of their pain. However, he was now beginning to see that their struggles were not just their own. They were intricately tied to his role in the lives of their husbands. And with every passing day, it became harder to avoid the reality that his actions—or lack thereof—were contributing to the unravelling of both marriages.

The more Omar thought about it, the more he realized how deeply intertwined his fate had become with theirs. He had always believed that loyalty meant standing by your friends no matter what, but now he wasn't so sure. Was he simply being loyal to a fault? Was he complicit in their self-destructive behaviours by choosing to remain silent and not speak up when he saw the warning signs?

In the stillness of his room, Omar closed his eyes and let the weight of his thoughts wash over him. Proverbs and old sayings flickered in his mind, as if trying to guide him through this moral maze: *"A friend in need is a friend indeed," "You are the average of the five people you spend the most time with,"* and *"Loyalty to a fault can become a chain that binds you."* He had always held onto the first two, thinking them to be his guiding principles. But now, the third one seemed to carry more weight than ever before.

Omar knew that he couldn't remain neutral forever. The truth was slowly eating away at him, gnawing at his conscience. As much as he wanted to protect his friends, he had come to realize that sometimes the most loyal thing you can do for someone is to help them face the truth, even if it means shattering their illusions. But doing so came with consequences. Telling Camila the truth about her husband and his addiction, or confronting Hamza about his wife's behaviour, could destroy the fragile trust they had left.

In cultures around the world, loyalty is seen as a virtue, but it is also tempered by the understanding that true loyalty requires honesty and sacrifice. In some traditions, *"A wise man speaks when he has something to say, but a fool speaks to say something."* Omar had always prided himself on being a good listener, but now, he wondered if staying silent had made him a fool. He couldn't keep pretending everything was fine when it clearly wasn't.

There was no easy answer, no clear path forward. But one thing became evident: Omar had to decide what kind of friend he wanted to be. Was he going to continue playing the role of the dutiful, silent supporter, or was it time to step up and tell his friends what they needed to hear, no matter how painful it might be?

He knew that facing the truth was never easy, but sometimes, as adages go, *"The truth will set you free."* It was time for Omar to figure out whether he could still save his friendships while also saving himself.

A Fractured Hope

Pablo had checked himself into rehab, but his stay was short-lived. Like a man dipping his toes into a river but refusing to wade in, he never fully committed to the process. At first, Camila had allowed herself to hope—hope that he would change, that the man she married would find his way back. But hope, as they say, is a double-edged sword; it lifts you only to let you fall harder when reality proves otherwise.

Pablo left rehab as quickly as he had entered, convinced that he had gained enough control over his demons. In his mind, he wasn't an addict; he was just a man who had lost his way temporarily. *"I don't need a program to tell me how to live,"* he had argued. But Camila knew better. She had spent nights watching his hands tremble when he thought no one was looking, heard his voice grow agitated when he was deprived of his vices. She recognized the cycle—denial, relapse, regret—on an endless loop.

She wanted to fight for her marriage, but she was running on empty. Work drained her, the burden of keeping their home together drained her, and Pablo's addiction drained her to the very marrow of her bones. She had thought about leaving, about packing her things and walking out, but the weight of expectation sat heavily on her shoulders. In her culture, leaving a marriage was not as simple as signing papers and moving on. A woman leaving her husband for "trivial" reasons was frowned upon. Addiction? That was a sickness, a challenge to be endured, not a justification for breaking vows. *"A woman endures, she does not abandon,"* her mother had once told her. But Camila wondered—how much endurance was enough? Did love mean breaking herself just to keep another whole?

Then came the moment that shattered whatever fragile balance she had been clinging to. She had discovered she was pregnant. For a brief moment, the world seemed to stand still, the chaos in her life drowned out by the whisper of a new beginning. A child. A fresh start. A reason to hope again. Maybe, just maybe, this would be the thing that anchored Pablo, that forced him to see what was truly at stake.

But life can be cruel. The joy that had barely taken root was ripped away before it could fully bloom. After only a few months, she lost the baby. No explanation. No warning. Just emptiness.

Grief settled over her like an iron cloak. She felt it in the way her body ached, in the way her spirit grew dull, in the way she could barely bring herself to get out of bed. The world kept turning, indifferent to her suffering. People whispered condolences, but their words were hollow, floating through the air like dried leaves carried by the wind. *"Everything happens for a reason,"* they told her. But what reason could there possibly be for this?

Pablo, in his own way, mourned. He drank. He partied. He numbed the pain in the only way he knew how, leaving Camila to grieve alone. He had never learned how to sit with pain, how to hold it, understand it, and let it pass. Instead, he ran from it, believing that if he drowned it deep enough, it would disappear.

Camila saw him slipping further away, and for the first time, she felt herself letting go. She had held onto this marriage with both hands, but what was she holding onto now? A ghost of a husband? A love that had long since rotted at the roots?

She looked at herself in the mirror one night, her reflection barely recognizable. There was a proverb from her childhood that echoed in her mind: *"A candle that burns for others eventually melts away."* She had spent so much time trying to keep Pablo from falling apart that she hadn't noticed how much of herself she had lost in the process.

TORN ROOTS, NEW BEGINNINGS

Something had to change. But what? And how?

For now, she had no answer. All she knew was that she couldn't keep living like this.

Pablo was sinking, and the deeper he fell, the more he resented the hands reaching out to pull him back. His addiction, like a vine creeping over a once-strong wall, had taken hold of every corner of his life. What had started as an escape had now become his reality, and he could no longer function without it.

Omar, seeing his friend unravelling, made a decision—if Pablo was going to use, at least he would use safely. The streets were dangerous, and bad batches had been taking lives left and right. Pablo didn't have the wisdom to be cautious, but Omar did. It was a bitter pill to swallow—becoming his friend's supplier—but at least this way, he could control the damage.

He didn't give Pablo more than he needed, rationing his supply carefully. It was an unorthodox intervention, but Omar knew that forcing Pablo into cold sobriety would only push him toward more dangerous sources. *"Better the devil you know than the devil you don't,"* he told himself.

But Pablo didn't see it that way. He hated feeling controlled. He wanted more, always more, and the fact that Omar was the one keeping it from him filled him with resentment. Who was Omar to dictate how much he could have? Who was Omar to stand between him and the only thing that made life bearable?

Yet, despite his frustration, Pablo also knew the truth. He had seen people overdose on laced drugs. He had heard the horror stories—people convulsing in the middle of the street, their lives snuffed out by one bad hit. If he cut Omar off, he would be throwing himself into a pit with no safety net. As much as he despised the control, he knew he needed it.

Their friendship had turned into a careful balancing act—one where every conversation was laced with unspoken tension. Omar was trying to save him. Pablo was trying to escape him. And neither of them knew how it would end.

Omar had hoped that bringing the issue to light would help Pablo see reason. Maybe if they talked as friends —just the guys, no judgment, no outside interference —Pablo would listen. Hamza, despite his troubles, still had a level head. If anyone could get through to Pablo, it would be them together.

But the moment the conversation started, it was like lighting a match in a room full of gasoline.

Pablo exploded.

He was already drowning in pressure—his exams were around the corner, and he could barely focus. Camila had been distant, and in his paranoid mind, he was convinced she was preparing to walk away for good. The walls of his life were caving in, and now his friend, the one he still relied on for his supply, was sitting him down for some kind of intervention?

He lashed out.

"You think you're better than me now, Omar? Just because you're the one handing me my stuff, you think you have the right to tell me how to live?" Pablo's voice dripped with venom. "Or maybe this isn't even about me. Maybe you just want me out of the way so you can go play house with my wife."

The accusation hit like a slap.

Omar felt his face heat up, his hands clenching into fists. He had done everything to help this man—to keep him safe, to keep his marriage intact—and this was the thanks he got?

Hamza stepped in, his voice calm but firm. "Pablo, you need to chill."

But Pablo wasn't having it. His eyes darted between them, seeing enemies where there were once only friends. He scoffed, shaking his head. "You're all in this together, aren't you? Everyone wants to control Pablo, everyone wants to tell Pablo what to do. You think I don't see it?"

Omar took a deep breath. He could see that arguing wouldn't get them anywhere. He had seen addicts spiral before—always finding a reason to push away the very people trying to save them. He had hoped Pablo would be different.

But tonight, Pablo was too far gone to listen.

Pablo stormed out, his anger like a raging fire that neither Omar nor Hamza could extinguish. They watched him go, knowing there was nothing they could say in that moment to bring him back.

Hamza exhaled heavily, rubbing his temples. "Let him be," he muttered. "We can't force him to see what he doesn't want to."

Omar nodded, but his mind was still racing. Pablo was unravelling faster than he had expected, and now, with all the resentment brewing between them, Omar wasn't sure how much longer he could even try to help him.

Hamza leaned back, his face grim. He had his own demons to face. He had recently discovered that Sara was also using drugs. The realization had hit him like a punch to the gut. He had suspected something was wrong, but he never thought it would be this.

And worst of all, Omar wasn't her supplier.

Which meant she had gone looking elsewhere.

That part stung the most. She had kept it hidden from him, just as she had hidden whatever else she had done at that party. He had spent years trying to build something stable for his family, working tirelessly to provide, and now everything was falling apart in his hands.

Hamza sighed. "I don't know what to do, man," he admitted. "Do I leave? Do I try to help her? I don't even know if she wants help."

Omar had no answers. He wasn't a marriage counsellor, and he wasn't the type to tell another man how to handle his household. All he could do was offer the simplest, most honest response he had.

"I wish you luck, brother."

And for the first time in a long time, Omar truly meant it.

The Breaking Point

They say *when the axe came into the forest, the trees said: "Don't worry. The handle is one of us."* In Pablo's case, the trouble was not from without, but within—and Camila had finally reached her limit. She stood in the doorway like a fortress—arms crossed, eyes cold, her expression carved with the stillness of finality. The silence between them was not the kind that precedes peace, but the hush before thunder.

"I can't do this anymore, Pablo," she said, her voice like a still pond hiding a storm underneath. Calm, yet final. *In every language, a heavy heart has few words.* She didn't yell. She didn't need to. Her words had the weight of judgment.

Pablo scoffed, stuffing his hands in his pockets the way a child hides stolen candy. "You don't get to decide that."

Camila's eyes flashed. There are moments when a woman's soul speaks louder than her voice. "I don't?" she said. "Pablo, I've been carrying this marriage like a pot of boiling water on my head, careful with every step, while you stumble around setting fires. I've begged, I've waited, I've watched you sink into yourself. But I won't drown with you."

Her words struck like an African drum—low and resonant, demanding attention. He felt the air grow tight around him. In his mind, *he was the man of the house*, the one to set the course. But *when a house is on fire, do you ask who lit the match or do you run?*

"You think you can just throw me out?" he barked. "Like I'm a stray dog?"

Camila didn't blink. *"The dog that barks the loudest does not bite,"* she might've said if her heart weren't breaking. Instead, she turned and, with the swiftness of someone who had prepared long before the storm arrived, placed his packed bag outside.

"I don't think," she said. "I know."

That was the end of it. Not with screaming. Not with plates shattered on the floor. Just the sound of a door—still open—but the heart behind it no longer was.

Pablo clenched his fists. His pride was like a brittle leaf, crunching under the weight of truth. This wasn't how it was supposed to go. *In his world, the rooster never let the hen lead the dance.* But Camila had changed.

She was no longer the woman who begged for peace; she was the one who had made it for herself.

And that terrified him more than anything.

With nowhere else to go, Pablo followed the only path that still held warmth. *In times of trouble, you return to where your feet first knew kindness.* He made his way to Omar's place.

Omar opened the door, his hair wild with sleep, his eyes half-shut. "You good, man?" he mumbled.

Pablo gave a laugh that wasn't really a laugh. "Not even close."

Omar didn't ask questions. *In some friendships, silence is the softest welcome.* He simply stepped aside and gestured toward the couch. "It's yours."

Pablo sank into it like a sack of grain—heavy, defeated, emptied out. He had lost his roof, his anchor, and whatever pride he had clung to. All that remained was Omar.

And somewhere in the deepest part of his soul, he knew: *If the same wind kept blowing, he'd soon lose that too.*

Omar had seen enough of life's bitter fruit to know he didn't want to harvest the same sorrow. *When the neighbour's house is on fire, a wise man wets his roof.* Watching Pablo unravel and witnessing the hairline fractures spidering through Hamza's marriage had been like holding a mirror to his own path. Destruction rarely announced itself with trumpets—it crept in silently, step by step, like dusk swallowing the sky.

It had once been easy to live as though tomorrow held an infinite number of second chances. But Omar had learned the hard way—*later is a promise life doesn't always keep.*

So that night, like a man returning home after a long journey through pride and denial, Omar arrived at Summer's apartment with her favourite takeout and a modest bouquet. In some cultures, flowers are an apology. In others, they're a symbol of renewal. Tonight, they were both.

They sat cross-legged on the couch, eating in a gentle silence. It was the kind of quiet that only exists between two people who have fought, forgiven, and still chosen to stay.

"I don't say it enough," Omar began, his voice softer than usual. "But I appreciate you. More than you know."

Summer smiled, but her eyes flickered—like a candle touched by wind. Behind that smile lived uncertainty. He reached for her hand, rough fingers brushing her delicate ones.

"I mean it," he said again. "I've been selfish. I've made choices I'm not proud of. But I see now, *a man who doesn't value his peace will soon live in chaos.* I don't want to take you for granted anymore."

Summer looked down, drew a long breath, and then raised her eyes to meet his. "Then you should know something," she said quietly.

There was a pause, brief, but loaded like thunderclouds before the rain.

"I'm pregnant."

And just like that, the ground beneath Omar shifted. The noises of the city outside melted into silence. The flickering light of the TV became as distant as starlight. The scent of food between them faded into nothingness.

"Pregnant?" He repeated the word, as if testing it in his mouth, trying to taste the reality of it.

Summer nodded slowly.

Omar leaned back, exhaling the kind of breath that comes after surviving a fall. His heart thudded—not in fear, but in awakening. *When the child is born, the man is born too,* goes an old saying from the East. And in that instant, he felt the weight and wonder of both truths crashing into him at once.

He had seen what reckless choices could do to families—to Pablo, to Hamza, to Sara. And now, life had handed him the first page of a brand-new story. The pen was in his hand.

He knew now—*you cannot plant corn and expect mangoes.* What he did from this moment forward would shape the kind of father, partner, and man he would become.

And so, with a trembling smile, he whispered the only words that made sense:

"Then let's do this right."

While Pablo wrestled with his inner demons like Jacob with the angel, locked in a battle that left his spirit limping, Omar found himself in unfamiliar territory—peace. Real peace. The kind that settles on a man like morning dew on grass, quiet but undeniable. His world, once paved with restless nights and the rhythm of danger, now revolved around something gentler, something sacred: Summer, and the child growing quietly inside her.

She was the first person to make him believe that he could be more than the sum of his past. *Even a crooked tree can grow straight if given the proper support*, they say in Kenya. And Summer had been that support, rooting him with hope, watering him with belief.

He was going to be a father. And that title—father—carried more weight than gold. He began to dream out loud in the soft evenings they shared, as though casting prayers into the wind. He spoke of school, of a real job, of a home not just made of walls, but of warmth and stability. He had never looked past the next hustle, the next quick fix. But now, every step had to matter—*when you're planting for the future, you dig deeper*.

Summer, always one to read the truth beneath silence, asked about Pablo every so often. Omar would shrug, evasive as smoke.

"He's still at my place," he muttered once, eyes on the floor. "Still trying to figure himself out."

But Summer knew. A woman's intuition, like the sea, is deep and full of unseen currents. "You've checked out," she said plainly, without accusation.

Omar exhaled—slow, weary. "I had his back, Summer. Even when he turned on me. Even when he couldn't see, I was still in his corner. But now?" He placed a hand over hers, resting gently on the curve of her belly. "I've got to put my energy where it counts. Into us. Into this."

Summer's eyes softened, her expression becoming something like sunrise after a storm. "That's all I needed to hear," she said.

For the first time in his life, Omar was choosing himself, not the streets that had stolen so many of his years, not the chaos that had masqueraded as friendship, and not even the bond with Pablo that had once felt unbreakable.

You cannot carry another man across the river if you're drowning yourself. Omar understood now: his path was forward, not backward.

His future had a name—Summer. And it had a heartbeat.

Omar's eyes were on Summer, the woman who had taught him that softness wasn't weakness, that love didn't need to be earned through pain. She was the stillness after a long journey, the home he never knew he was searching for.

TORN ROOTS, NEW BEGINNINGS

In a moment without fanfare or foresight, the question escaped his lips, as natural as breathing.

"Do you think I could be your husband?"

No ring. No kneeling. No fireworks or violins. Just a man laying his heart bare, as open and raw as a wound in the sun. Words from the soul need no dressing—they arrive like whispers from God.

Summer turned toward him, her face lit with a tenderness that only truth can summon. A slow smile stretched across her lips, which held joy, certainty, and something ancient—like she had known all along.

"I can't wait to be your wife," she said, her voice barely above a whisper, but it echoed in his bones like a sacred vow.

That was it. No elaborate promises, no crowd of witnesses. Just two souls meeting where love lives—*in the quiet, in the real, in the now.*

Suddenly overcome, Summer stood, her excitement as bright as the morning sun. "I need to call my mom," she beamed, phone in hand as she slipped outside.

Omar's chest filled with something unfamiliar—something holy. Not adrenaline. Not escape.

It was peace.

When a man finds his path, even chaos steps aside to let him pass. For the first time in his life, Omar wasn't just surviving. He was building—brick by brick, heartbeat by heartbeat—something lasting. Something true.

Something that looked a lot like forever.

Back at his apartment, Omar knew the hour had come. *A friend who stays silent while you burn is no friend at all.* If he genuinely cared for Pablo, he had to speak, not out of anger, but out of love. And love, as the elders say, sometimes wears the face of truth.

He found Pablo sunk deep into the couch, his face drawn like old leather, eyes red from days of shouting, sleepless nights, and the slow poison of regret. When their eyes met, Pablo's expression stiffened like a wall bracing for impact—but he said nothing.

Omar didn't flinch. He sat across from him, calm but firm. His voice, low and steady, was that of a man who had carried both silence and storms.

"Pablo," he began, "I've kept quiet for too long. But enough is enough. I'm disappointed, hermano."

Pablo bristled. "Disappointed? What's that supposed to mean?"

"It means you're throwing diamonds into the dirt and wondering why your hands are bleeding." Omar's voice sharpened. "Camila brought you here. She's the reason you had a shot at a better life. And now? You're risking it all over pride, over ego, over demons you refuse to fight."

Pablo shifted, his pride rising like heat off the pavement. But Omar didn't let up. *"A man who cannot be corrected is a man headed for the ditch,"* he said, echoing a saying his grandmother used to mutter when boys got too big for their shoes.

"I'm not saying you're not hurting. We all carry our battles. But she's been your rock. And you? You're turning your back on the one person who stood by you when no one else did."

Pablo opened his mouth to argue, but Omar raised a hand, firm like a father settling a restless son. "Just listen."

He leaned forward, voice softening but losing none of its edge. "You think love means never being challenged? No, hermano. Love is the woman who still cooked when you came home high. Who still held your hand when your words turned bitter. Who believed in you when even you didn't."

Omar let the silence hang for a beat.

"He who carries water should remember who dug the well. Any decent man would see that. Would honour that. Not with flowers and apologies, but with change."

Pablo's face twitched—somewhere between shame and defiance. But there was no fight left in him. Only a heavy stillness.

"You want to keep your family?" Omar asked, voice barely above a whisper now. "Then act like a man, not a wounded boy with something to prove."

Pablo slumped, the air in his lungs suddenly too heavy to hold. Guilt and truth sat with him, uninvited but undeniable.

Omar stood, pausing only to say, *"When the house is on fire, don't waste time blaming the wind.* Fix it. Before there's nothing left to save."

And with that, he left Pablo alone—with nothing but the truth, and the chance to finally do right by it.

TORN ROOTS, NEW BEGINNINGS

The air between them hung heavy, thick with the kind of silence that only comes after truth has been spoken aloud. Omar had done what most friends wouldn't: he'd laid Pablo bare. But the battle wasn't over—not with words, anyway. Pablo sat like a statue cracking at the edges, his pride still fighting a war his heart had already lost.

Omar saw it—the way Pablo's hands fidgeted, the way his jaw clenched just to stop it from trembling. He wasn't ready to speak. Maybe he never would be. But someone had to light the first match if there would ever be a way out of this darkness.

After nearly an hour of wrestling with the silence, Omar cleared his throat. "Can I call Camila?" he asked gently. "Can I talk to her—for you?"

Pablo's eyes narrowed. It was instinctual, like a wounded animal bracing for more pain. But the fire in them had dimmed. He nodded. "Fine," he said, barely above a whisper. "But you know she won't believe me."

Omar didn't answer. He just stepped outside, where the evening breeze could cut through the heat still clinging to his skin, and pulled out his phone to call Camila.

It rang. Once. Twice. Then her voice—familiar, but strained.

"Omar?"

"Camila," he said, his voice steady but threaded with urgency. "I'm with Pablo. He's not okay—but he wants to be. He wants to make things right."

A pause. Her silence held more pain than words ever could.

"What do you mean?" she asked finally, her voice fragile but sharp around the edges.

"He's ready to go back to rehab," Omar said. "He's ready to fight for his marriage. He knows he's messed up. He's not good with words right now—but I'm telling you, he wants this."

There was another long pause. He could almost hear her trying not to believe him, trying not to let hope sneak in.

"Omar… how do I know he means it?" she asked, her voice cracking ever so slightly. "I've been here before. Promises don't mean anything without change."

Omar nodded, even though she couldn't see it. "I know. But he's sitting here with nothing left. Not excuses. Not anger. Just regret. I had to be the one to speak because he couldn't. But I see it in him—he's tired of the cycle."

A silence stretched between them, but this one felt different. Softer. Like something in her had started to thaw.

"If he's serious…" she began, slowly, "he needs to show it. I can't go through this again."

"He will," Omar said. "He knows what's at stake now. He's ready to go tonight if he has to."

Camila's voice came back, low but resolute. "Okay. I'll speak to him."

Omar let out a breath he didn't know he'd been holding. "Thank you, Camila." He turned and stepped back inside, where Pablo sat like a man waiting for judgment.

"She wants to talk to you," Omar said gently, handing him the phone.

Pablo took it with trembling fingers. The phone felt heavy, like it carried everything he'd lost and everything he might still have.

"Camila..." he began, his voice rough with shame, "I'm sorry. For all of it. I want to fix this. I'll go back to rehab. I'll do whatever it takes. I just... I don't want to lose you."

There was a pause—long enough to crush a weaker man.

Then: "Pablo... if you're serious, prove it. You can come home, but you leave for rehab right after. No more lies. I'm giving you this chance because I still believe in you. But this is it."

"I understand," Pablo said, tears welling in his eyes. "I won't let you down again."

"I'll be waiting," she replied. And then the line went dead.

Pablo sat still, the phone cradled in his lap. He looked up at Omar with eyes that had seen too much pain— and just enough light.

"She's giving you a shot," Omar said softly. "Now it's your move."

TORN ROOTS, NEW BEGINNINGS

Pablo nodded slowly. "I won't mess this up," he whispered. "Not this time."

And as he rose from the couch, shoulders a little straighter, breath a little deeper, Omar saw something in him he hadn't seen in a long time—hope. Wounded, flickering, fragile… but real.

And sometimes, *real* is all it takes to begin again.

A Not-So-Clean Break

Omar had come to a crossroads where the heart speaks louder than the pocket, and the soul weighs heavier than the gold in one's hand. As the Swahili say, *"He who does not travel thinks his mother is the best cook."* Omar had seen enough of the world to know better now. The fast life had its sparkle, but even diamonds cut too deeply when pressed to the skin. With a child on the way, he no longer saw street hustle as a hustle, but a chain—shiny, yes, but still a chain.

They say, *"You can't plant a tree in the middle of a storm and expect it to take root."* Omar wanted his child to grow in calm soil, not among the thorns of late-night knocks and whispered deals. He understood that exiting the underworld was no simple matter. Leaving the game was not just quitting a job—it was stepping away from brothers, protectors, and enforcers who didn't tolerate silence unless it was sealed by respect... or blood.

He arranged a meeting. Neutral ground, a restaurant where hot tempers could cool over cold drinks. As he waited, nerves danced in his belly like ants on a sugar cube. He knew full well that in the underworld, there are only three exits: steel bars, a pine box, or walking away under a blessing cloaked in a threat.

The men arrived. Their silence was louder than a drumbeat, but their eyes told tales—some filled with sadness, others with calculation. Omar had once been the golden boy who handled business with clean hands and a clear head. If life were a game of chess, Omar had always moved like a knight—indirect but always decisive.

The meal passed in measured bites. Finally, one of the elders, his face like carved wood and eyes sharp as razors, broke the silence.

"So," he said slowly, "you're really hanging your boots?"

Omar gave a single nod. "Yes. I just got married this morning, and she's expecting. I think my child deserves a father, not a memory, not a martyr. I want them to see me grow old."

There were murmurs. One of the younger men scoffed softly. Another rubbed his hands together like trying to warm an old truth.

"You know the rules," said another, his tone cold but not cruel. "You don't just walk out of the lion's den without first feeding the lion."

Omar leaned forward. "I'm not a threat. I won't sing, I won't sell, I won't speak. My lips are sealed tighter than a drum in Ramadan. I just want peace. I'm not asking for a favour—I'm asking for release."

For a moment, time stretched like warm toffee in the sun. Then the eldest among them, the one with the final word, exhaled slowly.

"You've walked clean in dirty waters. Never dipped your fingers where they didn't belong. You've kept our trust, and that's more than most can say."

He paused, letting the weight of his words sink like an anchor.

"You can go. But if your tongue slips or trouble comes because of your name, we won't knock twice. And your family will feel the echo of your sins."

Omar didn't blink. *"A man who fears death dies every day,"* he thought to himself, and then said aloud: "Understood."

The old man nodded. "Then let this be the last bread we break."

And just like that, the atmosphere softened, like rain after a long drought. A few shook his hand. Others gave him slaps on the back. One leaned in and whispered, *"A good man never forgets the road that carried him—just don't walk it again."*

Omar was just a step away from the door when fate, like a lion waiting in the tall grass, pounced.

The restaurant's front doors exploded open with the fury of a thunderclap. Like a monsoon hitting dry land, chaos flooded the room. Officers in full tactical gear stormed in, voices sharp as razors:
"Hands where we can see them! Nobody move!"

Red and blue lights painted the dim room like a fever dream. Chairs scraped against the floor like desperate pleas. Glass shattered, a symbol of broken peace. Somewhere, someone gasped. The sounds were not unlike war drums—rhythmic, loud, and ominous.

Omar's legs twitched with the instinct to flee—*"feet that cannot stay still bring trouble,"* his grandmother used to say—but he resisted. To run would be to wear guilt like a second skin. So, like a tree in a storm, he stood tall and unmoving, raising his hands with measured grace.

His eyes darted to the men with whom he had just shared a final meal. Not one flinched. Their calmness was unsettling, like monks in a temple used to earthquakes. Clearly, this was not their first brush with the law's sharp edge.

A sergeant's voice cut through the tension like a machete through sugarcane, "We have warrants for multiple individuals connected to organized crime! Stay in your seats!"

Omar's stomach turned, caught in the tall grass, trampled by beasts of a world he had just walked away from.

One of the older mobsters leaned toward him, voice low but firm, like the steady beat of a village drum, "Don't say a word, kid," he whispered. "Our lawyer will take care of everything."

"A closed mouth catches no flies," Omar reminded himself. He gave a tight nod. Speaking now would be like lighting a match in a room full of kerosene.

The officers moved like wolves through the restaurant, snatching IDs, comparing faces with the cold certainty of hunters. Men were cuffed without ceremony, their fates sealed in ink long before tonight's meal. When they reached Omar, the officer squinted at his ID like it told half a story.

"Omar Al-Masri," he read aloud, flipping through a notepad. "No active warrant... but he's with them."

Another officer joined him, eyes scanning the list, "Take him in. We'll sort it out later."

Omar clenched his jaw. *"Even if you wash your hands, people still see the blood,"* the Turks say. He had done everything right—declared his peace, stepped away from the fire—and yet the flames licked at his heels.

Cold metal wrapped around his wrists like a serpent. He glanced back, catching the eyes of the elder who had warned him. The man gave him a slow nod—part blessing, part warning.

"Keep your mouth shut, and you'll walk."

And now, cuffed and cornered, he understood—*you can leave the life, but the life doesn't always leave you.*

Still, he kept silent. The wheel had turned, and he would ride it out. After all, *"a man who endures the storm earns the calm."*

At the police station, Omar sat on the cold, iron bench, his back against the concrete wall that had more cracks than a broken promise. The chill of the cell seeped into his bones like winter through an old window. Around him, silence hung thick—only the occasional distant clank of keys or murmur of guards punctuated the stillness.

The real gangsters—the wolves in tailored suits—had already walked free. Their lawyers, slicker than oiled ropes, had slipped through the system's loopholes with ease. Meanwhile, Omar remained, like a lamb caught in a lion's snare.

"He who rides on the devil's back must one day pay the fare," he thought bitterly. The music had stopped, and like a fool left standing in a game of musical chairs, he was the one without a seat.

The weight on his chest felt like a boulder—*"the heart of a man is a basket; the more you carry, the deeper it sinks,"* his mother once said. Jail, he could stomach. A trial, he could fight. But how could he face Summer? How could he tell the woman carrying his child that he might not be there when their baby takes its first breath?

The shame sat in his throat like a stone. Back home, his family had placed their dreams on his shoulders like garlands on a groom. He was the golden son, the one meant to lift generations from the grip of hardship. And now? Just another name on a docket. Just another son swallowed by the concrete belly of the justice system.

His one phone call lingered like an unopened door. But who could he call?

Hamza's world was crumbling like a sandcastle in high tide. Pablo, though recently reconciled, still burned with the wild fire of unpredictability. Omar's thoughts turned in circles, chasing hope like a dog chasing its tail.

And now, truly and deeply, he tasted the bitter fruit of solitude. Not the kind that came from being physically alone, but the kind that comes when your soul aches with burdens no one else can carry. Loneliness, he realized, wasn't about proximity. It was about despair with no one to confess it to.

So, he did what the old men used to do back home when storms came and the power went out—he sat. Quiet, still, and waiting for the dawn.

In the silence, he found no comfort, but he found clarity.

He could not change what had passed, nor could he rush what was to come. But he could, for now, bear it.

"When the axe forgets, the tree remembers." He would remember this—this silence, this cell, this stillness—and one day, when freedom returned, he would make it count.

Omar drew a long, slow breath, his hands balled into fists, knuckles white under the flickering light of the jail cell. The silence around him was thick, like molasses in winter, and the walls felt as if they were closing in, whispering every regret back to him.

"A man cannot carry two baskets on one shoulder," the old saying from his grandmother's village echoed in his mind. And now, faced with the impossible choice between the woman he loved and the family that raised him, he knew the time had come to choose.

Summer was his dawn—his second chance, his softness in a world made hard. She was the balm to his wounds, the soil in which he hoped to plant new roots. But his family? They were the tree from which he had fallen. Their hands had shaped his path, their sacrifices etched into his every step.

"The river that forgets its source will dry in the sun." He could never forget where he came from.

TORN ROOTS, NEW BEGINNINGS

The guilt sat heavy on his chest, like an old debt finally called in. He had promised Summer the moon and stars, but all he had given her was shadow and storm. She had offered him her trust, her body, her future—and now, a child. And what had he offered in return? Uncertainty. Fear. A life on the edge, now hanging by a thread.

He clenched his teeth. *"You cannot eat soup with a fork,"* he thought. Love alone could not dig him out of this hole. He needed freedom, and freedom needed strategy.

There was no room for hesitation. If he had to bend the truth like a reed in the wind, so be it. If he had to knock on old doors, cash in favours buried like bones beneath the surface, he would. *"In war, even the snake is a friend if it bites your enemy."*

Better to break one heart than to bury a dozen.

Summer was strong. She would ache, yes. But she would rise. *"A woman is like a teabag—you never know how strong she is until she's in hot water,"* as the saying goes. His mother? His siblings? They wouldn't recover. They needed him, not as a memory or a martyr, but as a man who could still walk, work, and provide.

So Omar swallowed his pain like bitter medicine and buried his feelings where no one could see them—deep down, behind steel and silence. *"The tear that falls inside the heart wets the soul but leaves the eyes dry."*

There would be no more room for sorrow. Only strategy.

He would find the cracks in the system. He would talk to whoever he had to. Say what needed to be said. Promise what needed to be promised. Even if it meant risking more than just his freedom.

Because the stakes weren't just his—they belonged to everyone who had ever believed in him.

And with that, Omar made peace with the storm.

He had to get out. No matter the cost.

Omar had always been two steps ahead, whether dodging trouble in the streets or slipping words through tight conversations. Quick hands and a quicker mind had saved him more times than he could count. But this? This was different. This was chess, not checkers. And the board was rigged from the start.

TORN ROOTS, NEW BEGINNINGS

They say *"a caged bird still dreams of the sky,"* and Omar? He wasn't just dreaming—he was mapping flight paths.

He watched. He listened. He played the fool when needed and kept his mouth shut when it mattered. A nod here, a joke there—guards were human, and humans got sloppy. Shift changes, smoke breaks, and blind spots in the cameras. Every routine was a crack in the wall. And where others saw steel and stone, Omar saw patterns.

"Even the tallest wall has a weak brick," his uncle used to say.

When the moment came, it wasn't loud. No alarms. No shouting. Just silence, and then absence. Omar moved like wind slipping through a crack—felt but unseen. He left behind a cell that still smelled like regret and sweat, and entered a world where every shadow was either a hiding place or a threat.

But he knew better than to linger.

The city was a death sentence waiting to be signed. Summer's name burned in his chest, but he couldn't go to her. Love was no shield against the law, and dragging her into this would make him the very thing he swore he'd never become—a curse on the ones he loved.

So he made the hardest call a man could make: disappear without a goodbye.

No letters. No phone calls. No trail.

They say *"a man who runs may live to fight another day,"* and for Omar, this wasn't just about survival—it was about redemption. He needed time, space, a new name, maybe even a new face. Because what waited behind him was a trap, and what waited ahead was a chance, however slim, to one day make it right.

The night he crossed the border, there were no fireworks. Just cold wind, a full moon, and silence.

And in that silence, Omar did what he had always done best.

He survived.

The Last Straw

Hamza had always worn his upbringing like armour—woven from tradition, faith, and a deep sense of duty. Back home, a husband's word was law, and a wife's virtue was measured by sacrifice and submission. There, drug use was a disgrace, a symptom of broken homes and failing morals.

But Canada wasn't home.

And Sara? She wasn't the woman he thought he'd married.

She said the drugs helped her cope. "It's just to relax," she told him, as if relaxation justified the fog in her eyes and the distance growing between them. But to Hamza, it wasn't casual—it was betrayal. A quiet erosion of everything their marriage was built on.

He asked her to stop. Pleaded, even. She didn't flinch.

"I can't," she said. Not "I won't." *I can't.*

That choice of words sank like a stone in his gut. It wasn't just resistance—it was resignation. And that made his blood boil.

Before he said something he'd regret, Hamza stormed out. The cold air hit his face, but it didn't cool the fire inside him. He walked for blocks, fists clenched, shame and rage swirling in his chest like a storm with no place to land.

He ended up at Camila's place.

Camila didn't ask questions. She opened the door, saw the storm in his eyes, and simply nodded. Her silence was a balm. She poured tea, let him talk. He ranted. He sighed. He broke down in quiet fragments. She listened.

By the time he left, his shoulders had dropped an inch, but the weight hadn't lifted.

When Hamza stepped through the door, he was greeted not by warmth or comfort but by the sharp, piercing cries of his daughters. The sound hit him like a blow to the chest.

"Baba, we're hungry," one of them whimpered, clutching her belly with trembling fingers.

TORN ROOTS, NEW BEGINNINGS

His eyes darted to the kitchen. Cold. Empty. No smell of food. No sign of care. Just a pot sitting in the sink, untouched.

"Sara?" he called out, trying to suppress the panic rising in his throat.

No answer.

He moved through the apartment like a man walking toward a fire. The bathroom door was slightly ajar, and a strange stillness seeped out from the crack.

He pushed it open.

And there she was—slumped against the wall, her head lolled to one side, eyes glassy and distant. A used injection, a rubber band, and an empty foil packet on the sink beside her. Lost to the high.

Hamza stood frozen for a beat. Then something inside him gave way.

"You left our children hungry... for *this*?" he growled, each word trembling with fury.

Sara didn't even flinch. Her gaze didn't quite meet his.

The rage ignited.

His hand moved before his thoughts could catch up. The belt came off with a snap. One strike. Then another. Her cry was barely more than a whisper.

But that wasn't enough.

The belt hit the floor.

His fists did not.

Each blow landed with months of resentment. Every broken promise. Every sleepless night. Every time he swallowed his pride and held out, hoping she would change. All of it poured into his fists.

He couldn't hear the children anymore. He couldn't hear anything. Just the thunder of his fury.

Until—

A scream.

High. Shrill. *His daughter's.*

He turned, dazed, and saw them standing there, frozen, their small hands over their mouths, their eyes wide with terror.

TORN ROOTS, NEW BEGINNINGS

They weren't crying because they were hungry anymore. They were crying because they had just watched their father become the monster he always promised he wasn't.

His hands trembled as he looked down. Blood. Bruises. Sara curled in on herself, whimpering like a wounded animal.

Hamza stumbled back, breath ragged, the horror dawning all at once.

What had he done?

He wasn't his father. He wasn't supposed to be this. But here he was—standing in the wreckage, surrounded by the sound of his daughters' cries and the silence of the woman he once loved.

The pounding on the door was distant—barely a murmur against the storm inside Hamza's mind. He sat motionless in the corner, staring at his hands. Bloodied. Shaking. Alien.

The weight of what he'd done pressed down on him like a boulder, each breath more laboured than the last.

The door burst open.

Uniformed officers flooded the apartment. One froze at the sight—Sara, slumped on the bathroom floor, barely recognizable beneath the swelling and bleeding. The children wailed in the background, clinging to each other like survivors.

"Sir, stand up!" an officer commanded.

Hamza didn't move.

They dragged him to his feet, cuffed his wrists behind his back. He offered no resistance. No words. Just silence.

As they led him outside, the distant wail of sirens cut through the air. Paramedics rushed past him. He caught a glimpse of Sara, oxygen mask over her face, limp on the stretcher.

He wanted to call out. To say *something*. But his mouth wouldn't open.

Then he saw her.

Camila.

She stood at the edge of the chaos, her face pale with disbelief. Her eyes scanned the scene—Sara, the crying girls, the blood on Hamza's hands—and then locked on his.

She didn't raise her voice. Didn't cry.

Just whispered, *"How could you?"*

Hamza couldn't answer. What answer could there be?

Sara was carried to the ambulance. Camila turned away from him, her expression hardening as she rushed to the children. She knelt, gathered them into her arms, whispering.

"Come on, sweethearts. You're coming with me."

As Hamza was shoved into the back of the squad car, the last thing he saw was Camila walking away, two tiny figures clinging to her like she was the only solid ground left in a collapsing world.

And in that moment, she was.

When Sara opened her eyes, the blinding hospital lights pierced through her skull. Her head throbbed. Her body ached. Every breath felt like a war she was barely winning.

The last thing she remembered was Hamza's face twisted in fury, the belt raised high, and her daughters' cries echoing in her ears.

A nurse noticed her stirring and quietly slipped out. Moments later, a woman entered—mid-40s, clipboard in hand, face set with careful compassion.

"Sara, I'm glad you're awake," she said softly. "There's something you need to know."

Sara gripped the blanket. Braced herself.

"Hamza has been deported."

The words hovered, weightless at first, then crashed down like stone.

"He pleaded guilty. Didn't fight it. Told the court he wasn't sorry… only sorry for wasting everyone's time. He said you had shamed him. That you deserved what he did to you."

Sara's breath caught. Not from pain, but from a deeper wound. A wound she hadn't expected to feel again.

No regret. Not even a flicker of it.

TORN ROOTS, NEW BEGINNINGS

Her lips trembled, but she didn't cry. Not anymore. She had cried enough for Hamza to last a lifetime.

"Where are my daughters?" she whispered.

"With your friend Camila," the woman replied. "She's been looking after them since that night. They're safe."

Sara nodded, slow and deliberate, though her throat burned with emotion. Camila. Always showing up when the sky collapsed.

Lying there, tubes in her arm and bruises painting her skin, Sara didn't feel strong. But she felt *something*. A spark, buried deep beneath the wreckage.

She didn't know what healing would look like yet. But she made herself a promise—quiet and fierce.

No one—not a man, not a past, not even her own shame—would ever hurt her like that again.

A New Beginning

Several full moons had passed since Pablo last laid eyes on Camila. In that time, he had wandered through the wilderness of his own making, finally choosing to face the shadows that had clung to him like a second skin. No one dragged him into the fire—he stepped in himself, knowing that to tame the lion within, he had to stop feeding it.

As fate would have it, the day of their anniversary found him standing once more at her door, a humble bouquet of her favourite blooms in hand. Flowers speak when words falter, and these petals carried a silent message: *I remember*.

When Camila opened the door—just a crack at first—her eyes were cautious, her heart guarded.

"I know I don't deserve a celebration," Pablo began, his voice measured like a man treading on a rope stretched over fire. "But I had to come. Not to win you back, but to show you I'm finally standing on solid ground."

TORN ROOTS, NEW BEGINNINGS

Camila, arms folded like shields over her chest, raised a brow. "And what, exactly, did you find on this new ground?"

He drew a deep breath, the kind that pulls from the gut. "I found that in trying to outrun my pain, I nearly outran my future. I forgot that a house isn't built by bricks alone, but by the hands that hold it up. You were those hands, Camila."

There was a stillness between them, like the pause before monsoon rains.

"I've been clean for months," he added, his gaze steady. "Not just dry. Clean. I want to build, not repair. Not patch. Build. A family, a life. Something rooted like an oak tree—deep and real."

Camila studied him. In the past, his words were honey without bees—sweet but empty. But this time, his eyes held the calm of a man who had walked through fire and come out singing not of pain, but purpose. As the Irish say, *"A good start is half the work."*

She didn't answer right away. Sometimes, the heart needs silence more than speeches. Then, without fanfare, she stepped back and opened the door just a bit more, *like dawn breaking after a long night.*

"Come in," she said softly.

Pablo nodded, and with the grace of a man reborn, crossed the threshold. One foot in the past, the other in possibility.

For a season, it seemed the storm had passed. Pablo and Camila found their rhythm again, like two dancers relearning old steps. They shared warm meals that tasted of comfort, whispered under moonlight like old lovers rediscovering their language, and even dared to speak of tomorrows not painted in fear. *As the Akan say, "By crawling, a child learns to stand."* Slowly, they were learning again how to stand, together.

But peace is a fragile bird, easily startled.

The news of Hamza came like a cold wind through a thin wall. He had been deported. Sara had come within a whisper of death. Their daughters, still so tender in age, had lost a father not by distance but by violence and silence.

The weight of it struck Pablo like thunder across a clear sky. He sat in stillness, eyes clouded, mind caught in the trap of memory. He knew the taste of addiction —the way it devours, the way it whispers lies in your own voice. And he knew the fury that comes when life slips out of your grasp like water through fingers.

TORN ROOTS, NEW BEGINNINGS

His hands trembled as he wiped his face, his voice no louder than the wind through the trees. "What if that had been us?" he asked. "What if I had pushed you that far?"

Camila reached out, her touch gentle as a prayer, but he recoiled, burying his sorrow in his palms. "I hurt you," he confessed. "I dragged you through the fire and never once looked back to see if you were burning."

His sobs came unrestrained, like rain breaking through a weak dam. *"He who conceals his grief finds no remedy,"* goes the Latin adage, and Pablo was done hiding.

Camila knelt beside him, arms circling his shoulders like a shawl. "You're here now," she murmured. "And you're trying. That's what matters."

He clung to her like a man lost at sea, finally finding driftwood.

"I don't deserve your forgiveness," he whispered.

She stroked his back, voice steady as a temple bell. "Maybe not. But I love you. And you're not the man who left. You're the man who came back."

In her embrace, he broke—not in weakness, but in surrender. At last, he let the past fall from his shoulders like old armour. And Camila, wise with wounds of her own, let him fall. Sometimes, a man must crumble before he can be rebuilt.

Pablo found joy in the most unexpected of places: *the sound of children's laughter and the smell of crayons.* At first, he walked carefully, like a man in another's home. He didn't know if Sara would want him there. He didn't know if the girls would cry or hide.

But children, like wildflowers, grow toward warmth.

At first, the girls giggled behind small hands. Then they took his fingers in theirs, demanded swings in the park, and asked for his help with puzzles that made his head spin. They laughed with the unfiltered joy that only children possess—*as if yesterday never happened and today is enough.*

Camila watched from a distance, her smile a quiet celebration. Pablo moved among them not as a visitor, but as someone *meant to be there.* Sara, still nursing invisible bruises, watched too. She said little, but her eyes, sharper now, noticed the changes. The old recklessness in Pablo was gone, replaced by something firmer. Rooted.

During one quiet evening, as Pablo helped with spelling words and crooked numbers, he leaned toward Camila and whispered, "I think I finally get it."

She looked at him, amused. "Get what?"

"That it's not just about surviving," he said, his voice soft, eyes on the girls. "It's about showing up for someone else. Not because you have to—but because you can."

She squeezed his hand gently. *"The heart that gives, gathers,"* she whispered, echoing a Taoist truth. "You just needed time."

Pablo smiled, watching the girls scribble and hum. For the first time in a long, winding journey, he felt like a tree that had finally found soil.

He was no longer running from the past. He was planting himself in the present.

And as the Hausa say, *"When the roots are deep, there is no reason to fear the wind."*

Pablo, like a man paying an old debt, insisted he was fine. Whenever Camila voiced concern, he would wave it off with quiet conviction. *"I owe you this,"* he'd say, as steady as a monk reciting a prayer. *"You carried us for so long. Let me carry us now."*

At first, Camila let him. There was comfort in the rhythm of it—coming home to the soft scent of simmering meals, folded laundry like temple offerings, and a home that breathed peace instead of tension. Pablo moved with the precision of someone who had counted their second chance like grains of rice—nothing wasted, nothing taken for granted. *As the Swahili saying goes, "Little by little, the bird builds its nest."* And Pablo was building theirs, one thoughtful act at a time.

One evening, Camila came home to the familiar clatter of dishes and found him meticulously plating her food, each detail arranged like a ritual. She stepped forward, placing a hand on his shoulder. "Pablo, you don't have to do all this."

He turned, the smallest of smiles tugging at his lips. "I *want* to."

"I know," she said, her voice warm but firm, like a mother soothing a fevered child. "But you're allowed to rest. You don't have to prove anything to me. I already love you—not for what you do, but for who you are."

Pablo paused, his shoulders stiff, the mask slipping for just a moment. "I just... I need to make up for everything."

Camila took his hands in hers, grounding him. *"Even the longest night is followed by dawn,"* she whispered. "You already have, Pablo. You're here. You've changed. That's enough."

He exhaled, a breath that seemed to carry the weight of a thousand unsaid apologies. And in her arms, he allowed himself, *at last*, to stop fighting shadows.

As the Persian proverb goes, "With patience, even an egg will walk." Perhaps, after all the storms, Pablo had finally earned not just a second chance, but peace.

One day, Pablo decided to look for his friends, but his search was like a man searching for a needle in a haystack, relentless, yet knowing the odds were slim. Time had carried Omar and Hamza far from his reach, each of them consumed by their own struggles, their own battles. The silence between them had become as thick as the fog in a dense forest, and the more Pablo searched, the more elusive they became.

Deep down, Pablo knew the futility of his quest. But there was a fire inside him—an obligation, like the weight of a promise made long ago. He couldn't let go of the feeling that he owed them something. Perhaps it was the debts of their shared history or the quiet understanding that in their lowest moments, they had been each other's lifelines. They had offered him help when he was lost, and now, in their absence, he wanted to return that kindness.

He reached out to mutual friends, scoured the depths of social media, leaving messages in the hope that someone, somewhere, would know something. His efforts were like casting a bottle into the ocean, hoping for an answer, yet receiving only the sound of the waves in return. The silence echoed, a reminder that sometimes, the past slips away, no matter how tightly you hold on.

His mind wandered back to the days when life had been simpler, when laughter had filled their late-night talks and their shared struggles had been lighter in the warmth of camaraderie. *As an African saying goes, "When there is love, there is no darkness."* Those were the days of friendship before the weight of the world had burdened their shoulders. And yet, even as those days seemed like distant memories, the guilt crept in. He hadn't been there when they needed him most. But *"What's past is prologue,"* as the saying goes. The past, while painful, couldn't be undone. What mattered now was what he could do in the present.

He thought back to the promises he had made—to Omar's guidance, to Hamza's steady voice amidst the chaos. Both men had faced their own inner battles. *"Each man is the architect of his fate,"* as the old Roman saying goes, and Pablo understood that better than anyone. Yet, in his heart, they were still his friends. They had been his pillars when the world had seemed to crumble, and no number of years or distance could erase that bond.

Still, despite his best efforts, there was no word from either of them. His phone calls fell into the void, his messages left unread, like a message in a bottle lost to the sea. Pablo clung to the hope that, somehow, one day, they would cross paths again.

In the quiet moments, when the world around him faded and only his thoughts remained, he wondered if they had found peace. *"Peace comes from within,"* said the Buddha, and Pablo prayed they had found it—whether it was in the embrace of forgiveness, the solace of solitude, or the grace of understanding. He couldn't be there to walk with them on their journey, but in his heart, he hoped that one day, they would find the peace they so deserved. And if fate allowed it, perhaps they would reconnect—and in doing so, heal the parts of themselves that had long been broken.

A Gamble for Redemption

Months had passed since Omar left the country, but the weight of his decisions still clung to him like a shadow. His escape from the law, though necessary, had isolated him from the world he once knew, and the echo of his absence haunted him daily. Summer and the baby had been his anchor, the reason he had hoped to change. Yet in fleeing, he had left them behind, and with that, he knew he had abandoned something precious.

"A bird in the hand is worth two in the bush," as the old saying goes, and Omar now understood the truth of that adage. He had been willing to throw away everything for freedom, but that very freedom had come at the cost of the future he could have built with Summer. Now, sitting in a dimly lit room in his small apartment, loneliness engulfed him. The emptiness was like the stillness of a desert, leaving him with nothing but his thoughts and the gnawing regret of what he had lost.

As the quiet stretched on, Omar's mind wandered to Summer, to the promise he had made her, to the future they could have shared. He thought of the precious moments he had missed or neglected, the birth of their child that he had not been there to witness. Omar couldn't help but wish he had acted differently—hadn't fled, hadn't let fear dictate his choices.

He hesitated, staring at his phone. The silence between him and the world he left behind was deafening. Yet, something inside him urged him to reach out, to check on Summer. His heart ached with the need for closure, to know that she was okay, that she had been able to move on in his absence. The road to redemption, he knew, could not be walked alone. "A friend in need is a friend indeed," the saying went, and in this moment, Pablo was the only connection he had left to his former life.

Finally, Omar dialled Pablo's number. The phone rang several times, each ring pulling him further into the abyss of uncertainty, before Pablo finally answered.

"Hello?" Pablo's voice was tentative, but familiar.

"It's Omar," he said, his voice shaky but resolute. "I—I had to know. How's Summer? How's the baby?"

There was a long pause. "Silence is the voice of complicity," a wise man once said. And in that silence, Omar could feel the weight of the news that was coming. Finally, Pablo spoke, his voice low and heavy with sorrow.

"She... she's been through a lot, Omar. I don't know how to tell you this, but... Summer lost the baby."

The words hit Omar like a punch, shattering the fragile calm he had built around himself. "When a man is in despair, even a single word of sorrow feels like a mountain." Omar's breath caught in his throat, and everything around him blurred into an indistinct haze.

"What... what do you mean? When? How?" Omar's voice cracked as the reality of the situation began to sink in.

Pablo let out a long sigh. *"Time, like a river, sweeps away all that stands in its path,"* he muttered, clearly struggling to find the right words. "It happened a couple of months ago. She... she didn't talk about it at first. But Camila—she helped her through it, helped her stay afloat."

Omar's hand trembled as he gripped the phone, a wave of guilt and sorrow flooding over him. *"To forsake a friend in need is to forsake your own soul,"* he thought bitterly. He had been so consumed by his escape, so focused on his own fears and regrets, that he had failed to check on the woman he had promised to protect.

"I should've been there," Omar whispered, his voice barely audible. "I should've stayed with her. I should've been there for both of them."

"I know, man," Pablo said, his tone soft but firm. "But sometimes, life forces our hand. The choices we make... they can't always be undone. You can't change what's happened, but you can choose what to do now. And you have to forgive yourself for what you couldn't control."

"It's easier to forgive others than to forgive oneself," Omar thought, the words resonating deep within him. He wanted to rewind time, to be the man Summer needed, to fix the pieces of the life he had broken. But reality, like a bitter river, flowed in one direction, and he couldn't change its course.

"I don't know what to do, Pablo," Omar confessed. "I feel like I've lost everything. I can't go back. I can't fix it."

"Maybe you don't have to fix it all at once," Pablo replied, his voice full of wisdom. "A journey of a thousand miles begins with a single step," he added.

"But you have to start, man. You need to talk to her. Let her know you care. Let her know you're sorry."

Omar nodded, though Pablo couldn't see him. *"The heart has its reasons which reason knows nothing of,"* he thought, understanding the truth of the words. "I will. I'll find a way to reach her. I just hope… I hope she can forgive me."

A heavy silence fell between them, and Omar could feel the weight of Pablo's thoughts as he spoke again.

"Don't wait too long," Pablo urged gently. "Life is short, and time slips away faster than a sandgrain in the wind. We've all seen how quickly things change."

Omar exhaled deeply, the weight of Pablo's words pressing on his chest. "A man who runs from his problems is like a farmer who abandons his field in the face of drought," he mused. He knew he couldn't run anymore. He had to face the consequences of his choices, no matter how painful they might be.

"Thanks, Pablo," Omar said, his voice now steady. "I appreciate it."

"Anytime, man. Just… make it count," Pablo replied, his words lingering even after the call ended.

TORN ROOTS, NEW BEGINNINGS

Omar sat in the stillness of his room, the weight of the world on his shoulders. He had run once, but he couldn't run anymore. The path ahead would be difficult, but he was ready to face it. For Summer. And for himself. *"The only way out is through,"* he thought as he stood up, determined to begin the journey of redemption.

Omar sat in the dim solitude of his small apartment, the weight of his choices pressing down on him like an anchor in deep waters. The silence around him felt suffocating, as though each breath he took carried with it a heavy burden. Time had passed—months, even—and yet, the ghosts of his past decisions clung to him, their sharp claws digging into his heart. Summer had been his north star, the reason he once dreamed of a better life, but shame and fear had kept him in exile. The life he had once hoped for with her now seemed like a distant dream, fading into the horizon.

But the time for running had come to an end. A man can only flee from his shadows for so long before they catch up. Omar knew deep in his soul that the life he had left behind was still there, waiting for him. His future, once bright with the possibilities of love and family, had slipped through his fingers like sand. He couldn't keep pretending it didn't matter. "The wound that cannot be seen is the hardest to heal," and Omar's wound, buried deep in his heart, had been festering in the silence of his isolation.

There was no escaping this anymore—not from the law, not from his conscience. Omar had left in haste, his departure fuelled by fear, but now he needed to return. *"One cannot live on borrowed time,"* his grandmother used to say. He had borrowed his freedom, and now the time had come to pay the price.

It wasn't an easy feat. Omar spent weeks crafting a plan, using the same resourcefulness that had once aided his flight. *"He who wants to cross the river must not mind getting his feet wet,"* and Omar's feet were already soaked. But this was no ordinary crossing—he was heading into the unknown, facing a past he could no longer deny. With help from a few trusted contacts, he managed to return to Canada, unnoticed but not unscathed. His first step, into the country he had left behind, felt like both a rebirth and a reckoning.

His first call was to Pablo, the one man he knew he could rely on in this storm. Omar could not carry this burden alone. He knew he needed a steady hand, and Pablo had always been that for him. Pablo wasted no time, reaching out to Camilla, who in turn connected them with a lawyer who specialized in cases of remorse and rehabilitation. *"Even the longest night will end and the sun will rise,*" and with their help, Omar began to chart the course toward redemption.

The courtroom, when the day finally arrived, was cold and indifferent. The echoes of his footsteps seemed to mock him as he walked in, a man who had once been free but had traded that freedom for fear and shame. *"A man who does not face the truth lives in the land of shadows,"* Omar thought. He was here, in this place of judgment, because he had chosen to confront his own darkness.

"I stand before you today," Omar said, his voice unwavering but burdened, "because I made mistakes—ones I've carried with me every day. I don't ask for your forgiveness right now. I only ask for the chance to make things right. To heal the wounds I've caused."

The lawyer, a sharp woman with a no-nonsense attitude, had built a case on Omar's remorse and his willingness to face the consequences. The road ahead would be hard, but Omar was prepared. The judge, after what seemed like an eternity, ruled in his favour. *"He who has committed no sin should cast the first stone,"* Omar reminded himself, though he was keenly aware that his sins were many. He was granted bail, with conditions, but it was a start. A glimmer of hope in a world that had once seemed so dark.

As he stepped out of the courthouse, the weight on his shoulders felt slightly lighter. *"The first step towards getting somewhere is to decide that you are not going to stay where you are."* That first step had been taken, toward facing his past, toward making amends. The road would be long, but Omar knew now that he had a chance.

Pablo was there, his presence a steadying force. "It's good to have you back, man," Pablo said, his voice firm but understanding. "Now you've got to make up for the time you've lost."

"I will," Omar replied, his voice steady despite the storm raging inside him. He wasn't sure where the road would lead, but he knew one thing for sure: He had to face Summer. He had to apologize, explain, and rebuild what he had destroyed. The past could not be erased, but it could be faced with the courage to make things right.

"It is never too late to become what you might have been," he whispered to himself, feeling the weight of those words settle in his chest. He wasn't running anymore. This was his reckoning, and he was ready to meet it head-on.

And so, Omar began the hardest journey of his life—not one of escape, but one of return, of reconciliation, and of a man willing to confront his past and build a future worthy of the love he had once forsaken.

Omar stood frozen on Summer's doorstep, the doorbell ringing out like a judge's gavel, signalling the moment of truth. His hand trembled as he gripped the doorbell, unsure if he was ready for the storm of emotions that might await him. The weight of the past several months hung heavily on his shoulders, each second stretching painfully as he waited for Summer to answer. He had hoped, prayed even, for a chance to explain, but he knew deep down that it was never going to be easy.

When the door finally opened, Summer stood there, unmoved, her expression closed off, a fortress built from the hurt he had caused. His heart dropped into his stomach, and he felt the familiar weight of regret tighten around his chest.

"Summer," he started, his voice shaky but filled with sincerity. "I'm so sorry. I know I don't deserve this, but I need to talk to you. I need to explain."

She didn't step aside, didn't soften her stance. She remained there, arms crossed over her chest, her eyes cold and unwavering.

"I don't want to hear it," she said, her voice barely a whisper, yet it cut through him like a blade. "You left. You disappeared without a word. I can't just pretend it didn't happen."

The silence between them felt suffocating. Omar's world seemed to collapse in on itself as her words sank deep into him. This wasn't the reunion he had imagined. She wasn't ready to forgive. Not yet.

He swallowed, trying to steady himself, but the knot in his throat made it impossible to speak without feeling like his voice was trapped. "Please, Summer. I know I messed up. I know nothing I say can undo the pain I caused, but I'm here now. I've come back to make it right."

Her face softened, but the hardness in her eyes didn't fade. "You don't get to just waltz back into my life and expect me to forgive you. I need time, Omar. I can't just move past everything like it's nothing."

Omar's chest tightened as he fought to find the right words, but none came. There was no quick fix, no magic phrase that would undo the hurt he had caused. He knew that now.

"I know you need time," he said quietly, his voice breaking just a little. "I'll give you all the time you need. I just... I just wanted you to know that I'm here. And I'm not going anywhere. Not again."

Summer didn't respond, but she didn't slam the door either. She didn't shut him out completely. That was something, a small glimmer of hope. Omar stepped back from the door, feeling like he had been rejected, but, at the same time, like a door had been left slightly ajar. It wasn't much, but it was a start. He couldn't rush her healing, and he couldn't force her forgiveness. He had to wait. He had to prove he had changed.

That night, as he sat at the dinner table with Pablo and Camilla, the silence was thick. They both had their quiet sadness, but there was a shared understanding in the air. Omar wasn't surprised by Summer's reaction, but the sting of rejection still lingered like a shadow over him. He hadn't expected her to embrace him with open arms, but a part of him had hoped she would at least listen.

Camilla, as perceptive as ever, broke the silence. "You know, Omar, I think you should give her space. You've done a lot, and this isn't something you can fix overnight."

"I know," Omar replied, his voice distant, drained of all energy. "I just... I thought if I came back, if I explained, maybe she'd understand. But I guess I was wrong."

"No," Camilla said softly but firmly, her tone steady. "You weren't wrong to come back. But Summer is hurt. You hurt her deeply, Omar. She'll need time to process everything before she's ready to talk."

Omar nodded, absorbing her words like a sponge. His mind had been running on overdrive, hoping that his return would be the key to unlocking forgiveness, but Camilla was right. Time had been stolen from both of them, and healing couldn't be rushed.

"For now," Camilla continued, her voice gentle but purposeful, "just focus on being here. Be with us. You can't rush her, but you can show her that you've changed, that you're committed to making things right."

Omar let out a slow breath, feeling the flicker of hope reignite within him. He hadn't expected things to be easy, but hearing Camilla's words reminded him that this was just the beginning. There was still work to be done, and he wasn't going to give up on it—not now.

Over the next few days, Omar did what he could to rebuild himself, not for Summer, but for himself. He cooked meals with Camilla, ran errands with Pablo, and filled the emptiness in his life with the steady rhythm of their routines. It wasn't perfect—nothing ever would be—but it was progress. He was learning to live in the moment, to find joy in the small things, to become a man worthy of the second chance he so desperately needed.

But even while trying to better himself, his thoughts always returned to Summer. She was never far from his mind, a constant ache in his heart. He wondered if she'd ever come around, if she'd ever see the changes he was trying to make. But all he could do was wait—and hope that when the time came, she would be willing to let him back in.

For now, he would bide his time, showing her that he wasn't the same man who had walked away in fear. He would prove, in every small action, that he was worth the wait.

And maybe, just maybe, she would see that he had returned not just for her, but for them.

The weeks after Omar's return were filled with a new sense of purpose that he hadn't felt in a long time. Camilla's advice to volunteer had opened up a new direction for him, one where he could begin to make amends, not by expecting anything in return, but by simply showing up and doing the work. At the addiction centre, he found himself surrounded by people fighting battles that mirrored his own—people struggling with their demons, just like he had seen in the past.

Each face he encountered at the centre reminded him that he wasn't so different from the people there. They were looking for a way out of the darkness, just like he had. And by offering his help, he was slowly beginning to heal, too. Every day spent with the people battling addiction taught him that recovery wasn't just about stopping a habit—it was about rebuilding a life, one small moment at a time. Omar knew he couldn't erase the past, but he could control his future. And he wasn't going to let his mistakes define him any longer.

The mechanical shop job was humble, but it was honest work, and it felt right. It was a step away from the life he had known and into something that felt more grounded, more real. Every evening, after his shift, he would head straight to the addiction centre. The work wasn't easy, but it gave him a sense of purpose.

When he arrived, he would dive straight into conversations, sharing his own experiences and lifting the spirits of others with his humour and natural charm. Omar knew what it felt like to hit rock bottom, to feel like the world was closing in on him. He had found a way out, and now, he wanted to show others that they could, too.

"Man, I remember when I was a kid, my mom used to make the best biryani," he'd say, his voice warm with the nostalgia of a better time. "And whenever she made it, the whole neighbourhood would smell it and come running. That's a memory you hold on to, you know?"

The people at the centre would laugh, and the room would lighten up. His stories sparked memories in others, encouraging them to open up about their own lives and the little things that kept them going. It wasn't always about the big milestones. Sometimes, it was about the small victories—the moments of connection, the shared laughter, and the simple joys that reminded them all that life was still worth living.

Omar didn't know if volunteering would ever be enough to undo the pain he had caused, but he was committed to trying. It was a long road ahead, but each day he spent helping others, sharing his stories, and showing up made him feel like he was starting to earn back a sense of purpose. He couldn't change the past, but with every laugh, every story shared, and every person he helped, he was moving closer to the person he wanted to be.

One evening, as he was finishing up at the shop, he received a call from Camilla.

"You're doing great, Omar," she said, her voice full of encouragement. "I can already see the difference you're making. Keep it up, and don't let anything pull you back."

"I won't, Camilla," Omar replied, his voice steady with conviction. "I'm not that guy anymore. I'm not running. I'm here, and I'm going to fix what I can."

He could feel Camilla's smile over the phone. "Good. And remember, Summer needs time. But she's seeing what you're doing. Just keep showing her, and one day, she'll see you for who you really are now."

Omar felt a surge of determination, a fire inside him that burned brighter with each passing day. He knew the road ahead wouldn't be easy. The time it would take for Summer to heal, to see the man he had become, was uncertain. But for the first time in a long time, Omar was on the right path. He had no illusions —it was going to take time, patience, and hard work. But he was willing to put in all of it.

As he finished his shift, he looked around the shop, at the steady rhythm of his work and the faces he was helping. He wasn't the man who had walked away anymore. He wasn't running. He was here, and he was going to prove that he was worth the wait.

It had been a few weeks since Omar began volunteering at the addiction centre, and with each passing day, he felt as though he was walking further away from the shadows of his past and toward a future he had once only dared to dream of. Each step—no matter how small—felt like a reclamation of his life. What had started as an act of atonement was slowly transforming into something greater. His stories, his laughter, and his willingness to listen were becoming a balm for the wounded souls he encountered. Though he did not know it, his impact was being quietly observed by those who recognized the potential in him.

One afternoon, as the sun began to set, Omar received a call that would alter the course of his life once again. The phone rang as he was getting home, the noise of the bustling city fading behind him as he answered it. It was Dr. Patel, a psychologist at the clinic where he was volunteering.

"Omar," Dr. Patel's voice was warm, full of conviction. "We've been watching your work here, and it's clear that you have something special. Your ability to connect with people, to make them feel truly heard and supported—it's something we believe could be revolutionary in treatment. Would you consider joining us? We want to offer you a position with our team."

It was as though the ground beneath him shifted, but as he processed the offer, Omar couldn't help but feel that this was the direction he had been meant to take all along. "When the student is ready, the teacher will appear," the old saying goes, and perhaps, just perhaps, this was his moment of readiness. It wasn't just about fixing himself anymore; it was about helping others, about making a tangible difference in the lives of people who, like him, needed someone to believe in them.

Without hesitation, Omar agreed to the position. His chest swelled with pride—not for the recognition, but for the chance to create something lasting. He had always been able to connect with people, but now, with the wisdom gleaned from his struggles, he felt equipped to guide others in a way he never had before. He wasn't just rebuilding his own life—he was building something that could help others rebuild theirs.

Just as he hung up the phone, a soft knock on the door interrupted his thoughts. He turned, expecting a pizza he had ordered on his way home, but his heart skipped a beat when he saw who stood in the doorway. It was Summer. The woman who had once held his heart in her hands now stood before him, her expression both hopeful and hesitant.

"Ah, the heart that loves is always young," but today, Summer's eyes betrayed a vulnerability Omar had never seen before. She stepped forward, and for a moment, neither of them spoke. The silence hung heavy between them, the weight of all that had gone unsaid.

"I've been meaning to talk to you," Summer began, her voice soft, as if the words were too heavy to speak. "I... I never filed for divorce, Omar. I couldn't. I couldn't let go of everything we had."

Omar's heart clenched as he realized that, despite his leaving, Summer had held onto the memory of their love. She was still carrying the hope that something could be salvaged. *"A tree is known by its fruit,"* the adage says, and Omar understood in that moment that the seeds of their love had not completely withered. They were still there, waiting for the right moment to blossom again.

Summer took a deep breath, steadying herself. "I know I've been angry, and I know I had every right to be. But I also know that the man I fell in love with is still in there. I see the changes in you, Omar. You're doing something meaningful now, something that matters. I believe in you. I always have. But I can't keep waiting for something that might never come back."

Omar's throat tightened as she spoke. The man she once knew, the man who had hurt her, was standing here now, vulnerable and regretful. "I'm sorry, Summer. I know I've caused you pain, more than I could ever make up for. But I want to show you that I'm not the same person. I'm ready to be the man you deserve. The man I should've been all along."

She smiled softly, the sadness in her eyes unmistakable. "I never stopped believing in you. I never stopped cherishing my wedding ring," she said, her voice tinged with quiet hope. She reached into her pocket and pulled out the wedding ring he had given her months ago, holding it out toward him. "It's always been here."

Omar's hands trembled as he took the ring from her, the weight of everything he had lost—and everything he stood to gain—flooding him. The love, the pain, the hope—it was all there, tangled up in the simple act of holding this small piece of metal.

"Put it back on me," she whispered, her voice filled with longing. "Let's start again. Let's take the next step... together."

TORN ROOTS, NEW BEGINNINGS

Omar's eyes welled with emotion as he slid the ring back onto her finger, his heart soaring and breaking all at once. The words he had been searching for escaped him in a hushed whisper. "I'm ready, Summer. Ready for everything."

She smiled, tears welling in her eyes. "Then let's begin this new journey together, Omar."

And in that moment, Omar knew that the road ahead would not be an easy one. But with Summer by his side, he was ready to face it. The path was uncertain, but with love, determination, and the lessons of the past, Omar was ready to walk that path, together with Summer, toward a future they would build side by side.

The Final Storm

Life, like the river that twists through mountain and plain, often surprises the traveller—sometimes with storms, other times with a clearing sky. For Omar, the tide had finally turned in his favour. After wandering through months of regret, like a man lost in a desert without water, he had found the oasis of love and purpose. The past, though scarred and heavy, no longer chained his feet. Instead, he walked forward with Summer by his side, hand in hand, dreaming of a family they once thought unreachable. As the Swahili saying goes, "Haba na haba hujaza kibaba"—little by little, the pot is filled. And so it was with their healing.

In the quiet of their shared mornings and the laughter of their evenings, Omar had stitched his soul back together. He had built something sturdy with Summer, like two carpenters working side by side to raise a home that could weather any storm. Their love was no longer fragile—it was tested, tempered like steel in fire. Together, they made decisions not as two people, but as one soul split between bodies.

TORN ROOTS, NEW BEGINNINGS

Meanwhile, Pablo, the friend who had once waded through his own darkness, had also emerged stronger. Like the Chinese proverb says, *"A gem cannot be polished without friction, nor a man perfected without trials."* Pablo had sat for his pharmacist exams and passed, a triumph not just of knowledge but of sheer will. He now stood at the door of a new life, one he had earned with calloused hands and sleepless nights. Omar watched him with quiet pride, knowing that they had all come far from where they once were.

But just as the sun shines brightest before the monsoon, peace was suddenly shattered. On an otherwise unremarkable afternoon, tragedy swept through like a thief in the night.

Camilla called. Her voice cracked, the kind of sound that told you something sacred had broken. "Omar... it's Sara," she whispered, each word trembling like a leaf in winter wind. "She's gone. She... overdosed."

The world around Omar went still, as if time itself held its breath. His heart sank like an anchor into a sea of sorrow. There is a saying in Arabic: *"A wound from a friend is better than a kiss from an enemy."* But this? This was a wound from life itself—a cruel cut no balm could heal. He had known Sara's pain, the demons she danced with in silence. But he hadn't known they would win.

Camilla sobbed, "She couldn't carry the weight anymore—the shame, the sadness. I should've seen it coming, but I didn't."

Omar felt hollow. He had been so focused on building something new that he had forgotten some old walls still hid cracks. *"When the roots are deep, there is no reason to fear the wind."* But what if the roots had never fully taken hold?

"I'm sorry, Camilla," he said, voice barely above a whisper, a lump swelling in his throat. "I should've done more. I should've noticed."

"The girls... they're going to be devastated," Camilla murmured. "I can't do this alone, Omar."

And like a lion stirred from slumber, resolve awoke in Omar. "You won't be alone. Not now, not ever. We'll get through this together. I promise."

When he told Summer, her eyes widened with sorrow, but she didn't speak—she just pulled him close, her embrace steady like the earth beneath him. "What can we do?" she asked softly, after a long silence.

"We have to help Camilla," Omar replied. "Help the kids. Whatever it takes."

TORN ROOTS, NEW BEGINNINGS

Summer nodded, her grip tightening. "We're family. And family sticks together—through rain and fire."

The news of Sara's passing struck like thunder on a clear day—sudden, jarring, and cruel. It left hearts shattered and minds spinning, but none more so than Camilla's. For her, grief arrived hand-in-hand with a mountain of responsibility. As she mourned the loss of her friend, her heart was equally consumed with concern for Sara's two young daughters. In many ways, Camilla had loved them as if they were her own flesh and blood. The African proverb says, *"It takes a village to raise a child,"* and Camilla had long been part of that village.

Now, with their mother gone and their father far away, the children's future hung in the balance like a lantern in the wind—uncertain, flickering, fragile. Hamza, reaching across distance and regret, had contacted Camilla. He asked her for two things: to help return Sara's body to her homeland, and to give the girls a life in Canada—a life of stability, opportunity, and healing. Like an old Turkish saying goes, *"A guest comes with ten blessings, but also with one burden,"* and the burden of this moment was heavy.

Camilla stood at a crossroads. The heart speaks one truth; the law often speaks another. While her instincts screamed to protect the girls, to shield them from more pain, she also knew that honouring Sara meant honouring her roots. Returning her to rest among her ancestors, as is the custom in many cultures, was an act of final dignity. The decision was not easy.

With the counsel of Omar and Summer, who had become like siblings-in-arms, Camilla chose the path of both compassion and courage. Together, they worked to send Sara's body home, where her soul could be at peace and her family could find closure. But the greater trial lay in the future of the girls. The law is often a maze without a map, and guardianship, immigration, and stability were all caught in a tangle of red tape.

"I want to keep them here," Camilla said, eyes weary, voice trembling, "but I can't make promises I might not be allowed to keep."

Omar placed a hand on her shoulder—a quiet gesture that spoke volumes. He knew the struggle well. Bureaucracy can be like quicksand: the harder one fights, the deeper they sink. But he also believed.

"We'll find a way," he said. "Even if it's one form at a time, one meeting at a time. What matters most is that they're safe."

TORN ROOTS, NEW BEGINNINGS

Camilla nodded, wiping her tears. *"The wound is the place where the light enters you,"* the Persian poet Rumi once wrote, and though her heart was bleeding, a sliver of that light had begun to shine.

Returning Sara's body was a journey of patience and persistence, but eventually, the arrangements were complete. Her family wept with gratitude. Her spirit, at last, was home. But even as her body found peace in foreign soil, her daughters remained between two worlds—mourning, unsure, and scared.

To help them bridge the abyss of loss, Camilla, Pablo, Omar, and Summer surrounded them with every tool of healing they could muster. Therapy sessions, warm meals, bedtime stories—little acts that stitch broken hearts back together. And together, they held the girls through the storm.

Camilla carried guilt like a shadow—unsure if she could live up to what the girls needed—but slowly, day by day, that doubt began to lift. In her quietest moments, she remembered an old saying from the Andes: *"They tried to bury us. They didn't know we were seeds."* Sara may have fallen, but her daughters, given care and love, could grow into something beautiful.

With the strength of community, the blessing of friendship, and the quiet fire of resilience, Camilla and her makeshift family chose to believe in a future rooted not in sorrow, but in promise. The road would not be easy—but then again, no meaningful journey ever is.

As the Zulu saying goes: *"Umuntu ngumuntu ngabantu"*—a person is a person through other people.

And so, through each other, they would rise.

In the days that followed Sara's passing, the house felt both full and empty—full of the quiet presence of her daughters and the echo of their loss, and empty of the certainty that had once anchored their lives. Camilla had opened her arms and her home to the girls, as one might gather fallen chicks beneath her wing, but even the warmest nest could not shield them from the winds of fate.

The tragedy of Sara's death had sent shockwaves through the lives of those around her, and now Camilla, Summer, Omar, and Pablo found themselves bound by duty, affection, and fear—all under the heavy cloud of legal ambiguity.

None of them had a claim to the girls, at least not in the eyes of the law. Love, though powerful, holds little sway in bureaucratic chambers. As time trudged forward, their conversations turned shallow, like a well run dry. The topic of guardianship hung in the air like a monsoon about to break, and none were brave enough to open the floodgates.

Camilla's affection for the girls was unquestionable, but so was her exhaustion. Omar and Summer stood beside her with open hearts but empty hands—without legal claim, their role remained that of caretakers in the shadows.

In quiet moments, they'd sit together, not unlike mourners after a long wake, with more thoughts than words. And in Camilla's mind, the conflict brewed like a pot left too long on the fire. Hamza, the girls' father, had rights. And though his past was blemished, the law, like a blindfolded judge, looked not to love but to lineage.

It was Hamza himself who broke the silence first, calling with a softened tone and a heavy heart. In his voice, there was no fire, only ash. *"A burden shared is a burden halved,"* he said without saying it, offering to bring his daughters back to his care and spare Camilla the weight of a load too great for one pair of hands.

"I never meant to make this harder for you," he told her. "You've done more than I could've ever asked. If you're willing, I'll handle their return. I'll buy the tickets, arrange everything. Just know that I'm grateful."

Camilla's heart clenched like a fist. *"When the child weans, the mother's heart still aches,"* and though the girls were not hers by birth, she had nourished them with everything she had. She nodded into the phone, a quiet agreement, though her spirit rebelled.

"Let me talk to the others," she said at last, her voice thick with sorrow.

That night, beneath a sky that seemed to mourn with them, the four friends gathered once more. There were no more detours around the topic; the time had come to face the truth.

"I just spoke with Hamza," Camilla began, each word falling like a stone. "He's sending for the girls. He doesn't want to burden us anymore. He's grateful. He's ready."

The silence that followed was long and heavy, like the pause before a storm breaks. It was Summer who found the first words, speaking gently. "It's hard, but he's still their father. And maybe this is the path that leads to healing."

Omar, always steady, nodded. "We've held the lantern for as long as we could. But now the road splits, and they must walk another path."

TORN ROOTS, NEW BEGINNINGS

Even Pablo, usually the quiet one, spoke with firm kindness. "You've given them a piece of your heart, Camilla. That's not something they'll forget."

Camilla felt her chest tighten, as if a hand was wringing her heart. "I just wish I could do more. I wish they didn't have to go."

"What the heart has once owned and had, it shall never lose," Omar said, paraphrasing a Persian adage.

The decision, like a blade sharpened by sorrow, was clear now. The girls would return to their father. It was not the ending they had hoped for, but it was one they could live with. In their hearts, they carried the belief that love, once planted, does not wither at the border's edge.

As they prepared the girls for departure, Camilla clung to a hope that danced like a flame in the wind—fragile but alive. *"When you nurture a child, your name lives forever."* And in every hug, every bedtime story, every moment of comfort she had given, her name had been etched into their hearts.

No matter where the road led them, she knew this much: they were loved, and they would never forget it.

It is often in the stillness of night that the heart speaks loudest. As Camilla lay awake, thoughts of the girls churned in her mind like waves on a restless sea. The call from Hamza had been the turning of a page—one chapter ending, another yet unwritten. She understood the need for the girls to be reunited with their father, for as the Akan proverb goes, *"The child who is not embraced by the village will burn it down to feel its warmth."* Yet, the idea of them leaving behind the life they had built in Canada gnawed at her spirit.

These girls, once strangers, had become as dear to Camilla, Pablo, Summer, and Omar as kin. Like vines around a trellis, their lives had intertwined. While love is not measured by blood, the law told another story. Still, Camilla believed that where there is a will, there is a way. She could not send the girls off like autumn leaves on the wind without anchoring them to something solid.

The seed of an idea had sprouted in her mind, and before it could bloom, she turned to Pablo. They spoke long into the night, the kind of conversation that burns slow like a clay stove in a West African kitchen—patient, deliberate, filled with the weight of purpose. When she felt the ground beneath her steady, she gathered the others.

TORN ROOTS, NEW BEGINNINGS

In the warmth of her living room, they sat as they often did—shoulder to shoulder, hearts bared. Camilla's voice, though calm, carried the gravity of one about to change a life.

"I've been thinking," she began, "What if we found a way for the girls to stay part of our lives even if they return to Hamza? What if we legally adopted them? We could adopt both, or one, and you guys could adopt the other. This way, they keep their Canadian status, and still be with their father."

Silence blanketed the room. The proposal hung in the air like incense smoke—unexpected but sacred.

Pablo, ever the first to lift the veil, nodded. "It's like giving them two roots—one in Canada, one with their father. They won't be lost between two shores."

Summer chimed in, her tone gentle. This might be the dawn we've been waiting for. As long as the girls don't feel like they're being torn in two, it could be the best path forward."

Omar, who had been weighing the idea like gold on a scale, finally spoke. "Families are not always born. Some are forged in fire. This... this could work."

With the group in agreement, the wheels were set in motion. Camilla contacted Hamza, her heart a drumbeat of hope and fear. To her surprise, he received the plan not as an insult to his fatherhood, but as a gift.

"I didn't see this coming," Hamza said, his voice thick with gratitude. "But it's the bridge we didn't know we needed. You've given my daughters something I never could have on my own."

Omar, placing his hand over his heart, replied, "Blood may be thicker than water, but love... love is the river that carries us all. This may not be a traditional family, but it is a real one. And real families walk together—through mud and honey alike."

As the adoption process began, each member of the group carried a piece of the burden. They weren't just preserving citizenship—they were preserving belonging, memory, identity.

In time, what once seemed like a broken road revealed itself to be a path paved with sacrifice, compassion, and the courage to choose love over ease. The girls would return to their father, yes, but they would do so with arms stretched across continents and hearts anchored in two homes.

And as the saying goes in many tongues and many lands—"*The child who is loved by many, grows strong like the baobab.*"

THE END.

www.ingramcontent.com/pod-product-compliance
Lightning Source LLC
Chambersburg PA
CBHW072012030526
44119CB00064B/638